Introduction

So you want to tour Minnesota, and who wouldn't? After all, it is the birthplace of the mighty Mississippi River. It's also home to the world-renowned Mayo Clinic, the Mall of America, 3M, and the childhood farm of American aviation hero Charles Lindbergh. Cheerleading, the black box and Spam are only a few of the creations invented in this Land of 10,000 Lakes. *National Geographic Traveler* included Minnesota's Boundary Waters Canoe Area Wilderness in its "50 places of a lifetime" list in 1999. And no one should miss the spectacular fall colors as the leaves turn from lush summer greens to brilliant reds and golds.

Minnesota Day Trips takes the information overload out of planning an excursion. Each chapter offers a number of attractions based on themes such as train trips, family days, romantic getaways, waterfalls and so on. Simply turn to the chapters that appeal and bypass the rest if you'd like.

For an overview of Minneapolis and St. Paul, take the 3½-hour guided tour offered by metroConnections. From a deluxe motor coach, you'll see the Skyway system, U.S. Bank Stadium, Historic Fort Snelling, State Capitol, Guthrie Theater, lovely Summit Avenue, residential areas and many more interesting sights. Call metroConnections at 612-333-TOUR (612-333-8687) or 800-747-TOUR (800-747-8687); www.awardwinningcitytours.com.

The Twin Cities have a metro transit system (metrotransit.org) that links many areas via bus, light rail and commuter train. Fares range from 50 cents to $3. Purchase tickets at vending machines located on station platforms. For more information, call 800-NEW-RIDER (800-639-7433) or 612-373-3333; www.metrotransit.org.

For more information about the Twin Cities, contact:

Minneapolis Regional Chamber of Commerce, 81 South 9th Street, Suite 200, Minneapolis; 612-370-9100; www.minneapolischamber.org

The Greater Minneapolis Convention & Visitors Association, 250 Marquette Avenue South, Suite 1300, Minneapolis; 888-676-MPLS (888-676-6757); www.minneapolis.org

St. Paul Area Chamber of Commerce, 401 Suite 150, St. Paul; 651-223-5000; www.s

St. Paul Convention and Visitors Bureau, 175 West Kellogg Boulevard, Suite 502, St. Paul; 800-627-6101 or 651-265-4900; www.visitsaintpaul.com

Minneapolis and St. Paul: Official Visitors Guide; www.visit-twincities.com

For information about greater Minnesota, contact the Minnesota Office of Tourism at 888-847-4866; www.exploreminnesota.com

Many attractions within *Minnesota Day Trips* include options of nearby things to see and do. There is also a select number of Western Wisconsin getaways. So go ahead and attend a Lion's Club pancake breakfast, or have yourself a heaping helping of hot dish at a church supper. Tour Minnesota's many museums and art galleries, hike the North Country or fish the River Valley's clear trout streams. Enjoy the land and that good old Midwestern friendliness Minnesotans are famous for.

Table of Contents

Churches 6

Duluth 12

Extreme Adventures. 26

Family Day. 34

Garden Tours 50

Geology & Cave Tours 58

Museums, Historic Sites & the Arts 70

Rochester. 78

Romantic Getaways 84

Small Town Antiquing 92

Trains, Trains & More Trains 110

Waterfalls. 118

Wine & Beer Lovers' Tours. 128

Odds & Ends 136

Index 152

Cathedral of St. Paul

Churches function as gathering places for those of like beliefs. The buildings are as diverse as the people they serve.

This chapter offers tours of Catholic churches rich in history and steeped in tradition—right down to the stained glass windows and pungent scent of burning incense. Marvel at the exquisitely crafted pews and confessionals, hand-painted statues and stenciled ceilings and walls. Domed naves arch to the heavens.

Most churches are open daily—usually until early evening. Use a side entrance if you find the front doors locked.

CHURCHES

COUNTRY CHURCHES

St. Boniface Church, *Hastings*. 8
  Option: Little Log House Village

St. Joseph Miesville Catholic Church, *Hastings* 8

St. John the Baptist Catholic Church, *Vermillion* 9

St. Mary's Catholic Church, *New Trier* 9

TWIN CITIES CHURCHES

Cathedral of St. Paul, *St. Paul*. 9

Church of Saint Agnes, *St. Paul* 9

Church of the Assumption, *St. Paul* 10
  Option: Mickey's Diner

The Basilica of Saint Mary, *Minneapolis* 10
  Options: Loring Park, Minneapolis Sculpture Garden

COUNTRY CHURCHES

1 St. Boniface Church

21889 Michael Avenue, Hastings; 651-437-2693; www.littleloghouseshow.com

Originally located in Hastings, historic St. Boniface found itself slated for demolition in 1995. Steve and Sylvia Bauer, owners of the Little Log House Village and Antique Power Show, bought the 1892 German Catholic church and dismantled it brick by brick, preserving the limestone foundation as well. They moved the materials, including the original stained glass windows, woodwork, light fixtures, pews and white painted altar to their antique village, then rebuilt the church to ²/₃ scale. Open only during the Little Log House Antique Power Show in the last full F–Su in July. Fee charged. Wheelchair accessible.

OPTION

Established in 1989, the Bauer's privately owned **Little Log House Village** comes alive annually during the last full weekend in July. See antique tractors work the fields as the threshers harvest grain. Belly up to the bar at the once bustling saloon, or watch the miller grind flour using waterwheel power. Explore old homesteads, an operating sawmill, a blacksmith shop, a general store, a schoolhouse, a butcher shop, a brothel, the Soo Line Depot and train, and old cars, machinery and tools. Stroll more than 40,000 square feet of beautiful gardens that were featured in the September 1999 issue of *Country Living* magazine. Take a walk or buggy ride over the world-famous spiral bridge (one of only three known to have existed in the world). Concessions; fee charged.

NOTE: Although the public may not enter the grounds without permission during the rest of the year, the village is definitely worth a drive-by.

2 St. Joseph Miesville Catholic Church

23955 Nicolai Avenue, Hastings; 651-437-3526; www.stjosephmiesville.com

Constructed in 1907, St. Joseph's was completely rebuilt after a devastating fire. Tradition is alive and evident in this village church, right down to the unmistakable aroma of incense and candles burning before patron saints. St. Joe's also has beautifully carved confessionals, wall stencils, hand-painted statues and a half dozen beautiful stained glass windows—including one in the balcony. Wheelchair accessible.

3 St. John the Baptist Catholic Church

106 West Main Street, Vermillion; 651-437-5652; www.stjohns-vermillion.com

This 1913 church has wonderful fluted columns, a half-circle choir loft, more than a dozen stained glass windows, a domed ceiling and ornate plaster moldings. A glorious trek into the past. Wheelchair accessible.

4 St. Mary's Catholic Church

8433 239th Street East, New Trier; 651-437-5546; www.stmarysnewtrier.com

St. Mary's is an imposing structure of red and white brick built high on a hill overlooking New Trier, a small village of 112 souls. The 1909 church is on the National Register of Historic Places and boasts an annual sausage supper right along with its mass schedule. Marvel at the unique curved communal rail, altar and side altars—all constructed of dark butternut edged in gold. The church has a domed ceiling over the nave and more than a dozen stained glass windows. Wheelchair accessible.

TWIN CITIES CHURCHES

5 Cathedral of St. Paul

239 Selby Avenue, St. Paul (across from the Minnesota History Center); 651-228-1766; www.cathedralsaintpaul.org

Cathedrals need not be grand—the only requirement is that they house the bishop's chair, or cathedra. However, the Cathedral of St. Paul is regally grand, serving the Archdiocese of St. Paul and Minneapolis. French architect Emmanuel Louis Masqueray produced the cathedral's modified Renaissance design in the early 1900s. (Masqueray also designed The Basilica of Saint Mary in Minneapolis.) Behind the massive altar, separate alcoves display hauntingly beautiful statues of several patron saints. Wheelchair accessible.

6 Church of Saint Agnes

548 Lafond Avenue, St. Paul (from the State Capitol, take University Avenue west to Dale Street, turn north; then 5 blocks down turn east onto Lafond Avenue, go 1 block); 651-293-1710; www.stagnes.net

This gorgeous 1912 German church with its crystal chandeliers and marble columns still offers Solemn Mass, complete with Latin chants every Sunday at 10 a.m. Wheelchair accessible.

7 Church of the Assumption

51 West 7th Street, downtown St. Paul; 651-224-7536; www.assumptionsp.org

Church of the Assumption boasts twin steeples and beautifully manicured grounds. Wheelchair accessible.

OPTION

Don't miss your chance for some tasty Mulligan stew at **Mickey's Diner**, located directly across the street from Church of the Assumption on the corner of St. Peter and 7th Streets. The red-and-yellow streetcar building was listed on the National Register of Historic Places in 1983. In business 24 hours a day, seven days a week since 1939, Mickey's long list of satisfied customers includes actors Bill Murray and Arnold Schwarzenegger.

8 The Basilica of Saint Mary

88 North 17th Street, Minneapolis (along I-94, across from Loring Park); 612-333-1381; www.mary.org

Built in the early 1900s, The Basilica of Saint Mary is every bit as impressive as those found in Rome. Designed in modern Renaissance style with a Byzantine treatment of the dome—that is, the church has a massive, lantern-crowned dome lifted from the substructure. The ceiling in the nave is 75 feet high and made of carved ornamental plaster. The stained glass windows depict the life of the Virgin Mary, to whom the basilica is dedicated. Wheelchair accessible.

OPTION

Pull up a park bench in nearby **Loring Park** for some great people-watching, or take a leisurely stroll through the colorful gardens. Tour the many interesting cafes and boutiques in the area, then walk across the footbridge to explore the 11-acre **Minneapolis Sculpture Garden**.

The Basilica of Saint Mary, Minneapolis

Aerial Lift Bridge and ore boat

A harbor town with a population of just over 86,000, Duluth offers tons of outdoor activities, art and museum tours, a zoo, train and boat rides, gardens and parks, America's only all-freshwater aquarium, live theater, a casino, great dining, shopping and so much more.

The twin ports of Duluth and Superior, Wisconsin, are the leading bulk-cargo ports on the Great Lakes–St. Lawrence Seaway. Lake Superior is the largest freshwater lake in the world and the final resting place for more than 350 ships, including the famous *Edmund Fitzgerald*. To help you get the most out of your Duluth trip, this chapter breaks down into several themes. Enjoy!

Duluth is 150 miles (2½ hours) north of the Twin Cities on I-35. Duluth Convention and Visitors Bureau: 800-4-DULUTH (800-438-5884) or 218-722-4011; www.visitduluth.com.

DULUTH

FAMILY DAYS

Duluth Huskies Baseball. 16

Great Lakes Aquarium 16

Lake Superior Maritime Visitor Center 16

Lake Superior Zoo 17

Minnesota Whitewater, *Scanlon* 17
Option: Jay Cooke State Park

North Shore Scenic Railroad—Pizza Train 17

Playfront Park. 17

Tom's Logging Camp 18

Vista Fleet Harbor Cruises 18

MUSEUMS & ART

Fairlawn Mansion. 18

Fitger's Brewery Complex Museum 19

Glensheen. 19

Karpeles Manuscript Library Museum 19

S.S. *Meteor* Maritime Museum 20

S.S. *William A. Irvin* Ore Boat Museum 20
Option: Haunted Ship (around Halloween)

The Depot. 20

The Old Firehouse & Police Museum 21

Tweed Museum of Art 21

Waterfront Sculpture Walk. 21
Option: Grandma's Restaurant

ROMANTIC GETAWAYS

Bay Front Carriages 22

Fitger's Brewery Complex. 22
Options: Fitger's Wine Cellars, Port Town Trolley

Leif Erikson Park & The Greenery Café & Bakery 22

North Shore Scenic Railroad. 23

Olcott House Bed & Breakfast Inn 23

Radisson Hotel Duluth—Harborview 23

Renegade Theater Company. 23

Skyline Parkway 24
  Options: Enger Park, Hawk Ridge Nature Reserve

Vista Fleet Harbor Cruises 24

Leif Erickson Park and Rose Garden

FAMILY DAYS

More than a shipping port or honeymoon retreat, Duluth is a great place for families. Kids and parents alike will love these fun and educational attractions.

1 Duluth Huskies Baseball

Wade Stadium, 101 North 35th Avenue West; 218-786-9909; northwoodsleague.com/duluth-huskies

Take in a ball game at the historic Wade Stadium, home to the Duluth Huskies. The team plays 36 regular season home games, facing tough opponents like the La Crosse Loggers. Jun–Aug. Wheelchair accessible. Call for season schedule and ticket prices.

2 Great Lakes Aquarium

353 Harbor Drive; 218-740-3474; www.glaquarium.org

The Great Lakes Aquarium features a unique 120,000-gallon display. Captain an ore freighter and learn about the unpredictable weather patterns responsible for sinking ships. Experience over 30 interactive exhibits including glaciers, lava flows and wave creation. Otters, frogs, fish, birds and mammals throughout. Changing exhibits and special programs. Open daily. Fee charged. Children 2 and under free.

NOTE: Separate fee for parking.

3 Lake Superior Maritime Visitor Center

On the waterfront in Canal Park next to the Aerial Lift Bridge; 218-720-5260, ext. 1; www.lsmma.com

The Lake Superior Maritime Visitor Center features full-scale replicas of ship cabins, recovered artifacts from sunken ships, film presentations, sightseeing information and posted arrival and departure times of huge 1,000-foot freighters that pass within yards of the building. Open daily. Wheelchair accessible. Free.

NOTE: For more shipping information, call the Boatwatcher's Hotline at 218-722-6489 (closed February to mid-March), or the Duluth Shipping News at 218-722-3119; www.duluthshippingnews.com.

4 Lake Superior Zoo

7210 Fremont Street; 218-730-4500; www.lszooduluth.org

More than 25 endangered and threatened species from around the world live at the zoo, including Snow Leopards, Black-Footed Ferrets, Bald Eagles, and an Amur Tiger. Primate Conservation Center, gift shop and cafe. Open year-round. Check website for days and hours. Wheelchair accessible. Fee charged. Children 2 and under free.

5 Minnesota Whitewater

3212 River Gate Avenue, Scanlon. Located 18 miles south of Duluth on the St. Louis River in Scanlon; 218-522-4446; www.minnesotawhitewater.com

Does your family crave action-packed adventure? Then take them whitewater rafting. Minnesota Whitewater supplies the equipment, shuttle service and guides you need for a wet and wild ride down 4 miles of the St. Louis River. No experience necessary, but must be age 12 or older. Daily May–Sep. Fee charged. Call ahead for a list of recommended clothing and gear.

OPTION

Jay Cooke State Park, 780 Highway 210, Carlton (eastern edge of town); 218-384-4610. More than 14 miles of scenic biking and hiking from Carlton to Duluth. The park's focal point is a swinging suspension bridge overlooking an awesome gorge. Keep in mind that the bike or hike back is uphill!

6 North Shore Scenic Railroad—Pizza Train

The Depot (downtown Duluth), 506 West Michigan Street; 218-722-1273 or 800-423-1273; www.northshorescenicrailroad.org

Enjoy a $2\frac{1}{2}$-hour trip aboard a vintage train as it rumbles over tall trestles spanning deep river gorges, but you won't have to ride on an empty stomach. This adventure includes Domino's Pizza and fun! Check website for days and hours. Wheelchair accessible. Reservations required by 2 p.m. the day of the excursion. Fee charged.

7 Playfront Park

Bayfront Festival Park at the base of 5th Avenue West (on the waterfront by the Great Lakes Aquarium)

Take a picnic lunch to the Playfront at Bayfront Festival Park and let the kids run wild. They'll have a blast on all the cool playground equipment, giving you a chance to put your feet up and relax. By the way, you're in a perfect position for watching giant ore freighters cruise into the harbor.

8 | Tom's Logging Camp

5797 North Shore Drive (16 miles northeast of Duluth on scenic Highway 61);
218-525-4120; www.tomsloggingcamp.com

At Tom's Logging Camp, you'll learn how the Minnesota loggers lived
and worked before the chainsaw. Try your hand at blacksmithing or
feed pygmy goats, bunnies and rainbow trout. Step inside the gravity
house and watch a ball mysteriously roll uphill! Open daily May–Oct.
Gift shop. Fee charged. Children age 5 and under free.

9 | Vista Fleet Harbor Cruises

323 Harbor Drive; 218-722-6218 or 877-883-4002; www.vistafleet.com

For a close-up view of a huge lake freighter, take a Vista Harbor
Cruise. They offer an interesting, narrated 1½-hour tour of the
harbor and information about the ships at port. Mid-May to mid-Oct.
Wheelchair accessible. Fee charged.

NOTE: Vista Fleet also offers a variety of cruises which include
meals. Call or check the website for more information.

MUSEUMS & ART

From gorgeous works of art, to the world's only historic whaleback freighter, to murder—Duluth's museums have it all!

10 | Fairlawn Mansion

906 East 2nd Street, Superior, WI (adjacent to Barker's Island); 715-394-5712;
www.superiorpublicmuseums.org

Tour this nineteenth-century Victorian, 42-room house, which was
once the home of lumber baron Martin Pattison. A 1998 renovation
returned the house to its original splendor—carved wood, marble,
silver trim, brass and English tile. Open year-round. Wheelchair
accessible on first floor. Fee charged.

NOTE: Tour guides are not all the same—some are energetic, some
are serious, but most are at least alive. Tourists have reported a
very pleasant young servant gal guiding them through the museum.
Trouble is, the servant gal is a ghost!

11 Fitger's Brewery Complex Museum

600 East Superior Street; 218-722-8826; www.fitgers.com

Fitger's is a Minnesota brewing legend. Established in 1857, it survived the Prohibition years by producing soda pop and candy bars. The museum specializes in northern Minnesota brewing history and memorabilia from what was once one of the most successful breweries in the state. Open when staff is available. Wheelchair accessible. Free.

NOTE: Fitger's Brewhouse serves sandwiches, soups, burgers and has its own handcrafted ales on tap.

12 Glensheen

3300 London Road (five miles east of downtown Duluth); 218-726-8910 or 888-454-GLEN (888-454-4536); glensheen.wp.d.umn.edu

Listed on the National Register of Historic Places, this luxurious, 39-room Jacobean-style mansion completed in 1908 showcases custom-designed furnishings original to the house. In 1977, an upstairs bedroom was the scene of the brutal double murder of heiress Elisabeth Congdon and her nurse. Congdon's daughter and son-in-law were tried for the crime, and the son-in-law was found guilty.

Grounds include formal gardens, carriage house with carriage collection, gardener's cottage and clay tennis court. Tours conducted year-round. Check website for days and hours. Wheelchair accessible. Fee charged.

13 Karpeles Manuscript Library Museum

902 East 1st Street; 218-728-0630; www.rain.org/~karpeles/dulfrm.html

Established by California businessman and Duluth native David Karpeles, the museum displays rotating exhibitions of historical documents from Karpeles' private manuscript collection. The collection, one of the largest private collections in the world, preserves original writings of great authors, musicians, scientists, philosophers, statesmen and sovereigns from all periods of history. Notable past exhibitions include original handwritten drafts of the U.S. Bill of Rights, the Emancipation Proclamation and Handel's Messiah. The museum's permanent collection includes Egyptian artifacts, and also model ships, including the *Titanic*. Closed Mondays and holidays.

14 S.S. *Meteor* Maritime Museum

Berthed on Barker's Island, WI; 715-394-5712; www.superiorpublicmuseums.org

Launched in Superior in 1896, the S.S. *Meteor* is the world's only historic whaleback freighter still in existence. Daily tours mid-May to mid-Oct. Fee charged. Wheelchair accessible only on first floor.

15 S.S. *William A. Irvin* Ore Boat Museum

350 Harbor Drive; 218-722-7876 or 218-722-5573 (Duluth Entertainment and Convention Center); decc.org/william-a-irvin

A floating museum permanently docked across from the Duluth Entertainment and Convention Center, the *William A. Irvin* was once the flagship of U.S. Steel's Great Lakes Fleet. It carried ore and coal for 40 years. One-hour guided tour of engine room, staterooms, galley, dining room and pilothouse. Open daily. Fee charged.

OPTION

In October the stately *William A. Irvin* morphs into a **Haunted Ship**. Beware—this bone-chilling experience is not for the faint of heart! Call the museum for ticket information, or go to www.duluthhauntedship.com.

16 The Depot

506 West Michigan Street; 218-727-8025 or 888-733-5833; www.duluthdepot.org

A must-see for every museum and art lover! Advertised as "everything under one roof," the 1892 Chateauesque-style Depot certainly has it all: Art Institute, Lake Superior Railroad Museum, St. Louis County Historical Society, as well as the School of the Minnesota Ballet, Duluth Playhouse, Duluth-Superior Symphony Orchestra, Matinee Musicale, Arrowhead Chorale and Veterans' Memorial Hall. Open daily. Wheelchair accessible. Fee charged. Ticket price includes admission to all four museums.

17 The Old Firehouse & Police Museum

402 23rd Avenue East (just south of Highways 2 & 53), Superior, WI; 715-394-5712; www.superiorpublicmuseums.org

The 1890s fire station houses vintage fire engines, a unique collection of toy fire engines, police and fire equipment, artifacts and the Wisconsin Fire and Police Hall of Fame. Mid-May to mid-Oct. Wheelchair accessible only on first floor. Free.

18 Tweed Museum of Art

University of Minnesota Duluth Campus, 1201 Ordean Court; 218-726-8222; www.d.umn.edu/tma

Contemporary and historical American, European and American Indian art is displayed in the museum's 11 galleries. The museum also is home to the Glenn C. Nelson International Ceramics Collection and the Potlatch "Mountie" Illustration Collection. The museum hosts approximately ten exhibitions annually. Gift shop. Open T–Su. Wheelchair accessible. Donation suggested.

19 Waterfront Sculpture Walk

Canal Park—Lakeshore Walk

A series of sculptures representing the social, cultural and historical values of Duluth and cities around the world create an outdoor gallery of international art.

OPTION

Have lunch at **Grandma's Restaurant** or, at least, take a peek inside at the interesting paraphernalia hanging from the ceiling and on the walls. Burgers, specialty sandwiches, Marathon Spaghetti, steak and more. Open daily; 522 Lake Avenue South; 218-727-4192; www.grandmasrestaurants.com.

ROMANTIC GETAWAYS

Whether you've been together 50 years or are just starting out, Duluth is the place to go with the person you love.

20 Bayfront Carriages

Canal Park across from Grandma's Restaurant; 218-428-9563; www.bayfrontcarriages.com

Take a romantic carriage ride along the waterfront. Bayfront Carriages (across from Grandma's Restaurant) offers their horse-drawn service on scheduled days; see website for days and times. Fee charged.

21 Fitger's Brewery Complex

600 East Superior Street; 218-279-BREW; www.brewhouse.net

Fitger's was a brewery from 1882 until 1972. Now a shopping complex with elegant dining opportunities and an overnight guest inn, learn about its history in the free museum. **Fitger's Brewhouse Brewery & Grille** features its own award-winning handcrafted ales, homemade soups, sandwiches, burgers and more. Wheelchair accessible.

OPTION

Stop by **Fitger's Wine Cellars** (within the Fitger's complex) and choose a favorite wine from their more than 1,000 vintages. • Fifty cents gets you a ride on the **Port Town Trolley** from the Waterfront to Fitger's. Wheelchair accessible.

22 Leif Erikson Park & The Greenery Café & Bakery

Leif Erikson Park is north of Fitger's Complex on London Road.
The Greenery Café & Bakery, Holiday Court, 2nd Level, 200 West 1st Street; 218-727-3387

Order a picnic-to-go from The Greenery Café & Bakery and head to the Rose Garden at Leif Erikson Park. One of Minnesota's prettiest parks, it boasts more than 3,000 rose bushes, a fountain and a gazebo, and many spots to enjoy the incredible views of the lake.

NOTE: Rose-blooming season begins in late June to early July.

23 North Shore Scenic Railroad

The Depot, 506 West Michigan Street; 800-423-1273 or 218-722-1273;
www.northshorescenicrailroad.org

The North Shore Scenic Railroad offers a special 2½-hour Elegant
Dinner Train excursion hosted by various Duluth restaurants.
Restored vintage train rumbles through the city along the rugged
shoreline and deep into the North Woods. Trip scheduled for
selected weekends only. Limited wheelchair accessibility. Call
ahead for reservations, menu and dates.

24 Olcott House Bed & Breakfast Inn

2316 East 1st Street; 800-715-1339 or 218-728-1339; www.olcotthouse.com
Also see www.duluthbandb.com for more information on Duluth's historic inns.

A 1904 "Gone With the Wind" historic grand mansion, the Olcott
House offers a choice of six romantic suites with working fireplaces
and private baths or a carriage house hideaway complete with kitchen
and living room. Sip a glass of iced tea on the Grand Porch before
going out for dinner or stroll the manicured grounds in the company
of your sweetheart. Wonderful two-course candlelight breakfast
served in your suite.

25 Radisson Hotel Duluth—Harborview

505 West Superior Street; 800-333-3333 or 218-727-8981;
www.radisson.com/duluthmn

Make dinner reservations at Radisson's **JJ Astor Restaurant and
Lounge**. Located on the 16th floor, the revolving restaurant offers a
spectacular harbor and city view. Full revolution every 72 minutes.
American cuisine. Wheelchair accessible. Dinner served daily.

26 Renegade Theater Company

Teatro Zuccone, 222 East Superior Street; 218-336-1414;
www.renegadetheatercompany.org

Top off your evening with a show. The Renegade Theater Company
offers mainstage productions as well as hilarious improv performances every Friday and Saturday nights. Call for reservations and
ticket prices.

27 Skyline Parkway

Take Highway 53 north off of I-35. Skyline Parkway crosses Highway 53.

This dramatic, 30-mile drive 600 feet above the shoreline is one long, breathtaking view of Lake Superior and the harbor.

OPTION

There are frequent observation points and markers, including the tower at **Enger Park**. Seven Bridges Road winds through forested hillsides and over seven stone bridges. Explore caverns, waterfalls and the **Hawk Ridge Nature Reserve**, which is rated one of the nation's top ten viewing spots for hawks; www.hawkridge.org.

28 Vista Fleet Harbor Cruises

323 Harbor Drive; 218-722-6218 or 877-883-4002; www.vistafleet.com

Enjoy scenic Lake Superior and the international harbor aboard the Vista Star. The 2-hour dinner cruise is especially popular. Wheelchair accessible. Call for hours. Reservations required.

Enger Tower

Voyageurs National Park

Minnesota's diverse landscapes and ever-changing seasons are not only breathtakingly beautiful, but they provide great opportunities for the adventure seeker as well.

For all of you who hunger for a different kind of a vacation—one that caters to your free spirit—this chapter is for you. From dairy farming, to mushing a dog team, to renting a houseboat, Minnesota is your vacationland for adventure!

EXTREME ADVENTURES

Boundary Country Trekking (Yurt to Yurt!), *Grand Marais* 28

Gunflint Lodge, *Grand Marais* 29

Harley Trip to the Headwaters 29
   Options: Bemidji, Lake Bemidji State Park, Scenic Byway County 39, Star Island

Rock Climb & Sea Kayak, *Duluth*. 31

Room to Roam Farm Vacations, *Fountain City, WI*. 31

Voyageurs National Park Houseboats 32
   Options: Vince Shute Wildlife Sanctuary, Orr Bog Walk

Wintergreen Dogsled Vacations, *Ely* 33

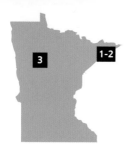

3 **1-2**

1 Boundary Country Trekking (Yurt to Yurt!)

11 Poplar Creek Drive, Grand Marais; 800-322-8327 or 218-388-4487; www.boundarycountry.com. Grand Marais is approximately 260 miles from the Twin Cities.

Advertised as "civilized adventures for the active traveler," Boundary Country Trekking is on the Gunflint Trail. They offer a variety of vacation packages for every season including mountain biking, guided BWCAW canoe trips, yurt-to-yurt fat tire biking (year-round), and lodge-to-lodge hiking trips on the Superior Hiking Trail. A popular winter trip is yurt-to-yurt skiing. (A yurt is a canvas-covered Mongolian hut with a round, peaked roof.) If you're into building muscles and sweat, sign up for a Work Weekend of clearing the Banadad Ski Trail of downed trees and brush. The trail is within the BWCAW where power tools are not permitted, so all maintenance is done by hand labor. Lodging, meals and tools are provided. For more information on all of Boundary Country Trekking's vacation options, check out their website or give them a call.

NOTE: The **Boundary Waters Canoe Area Wilderness** (BWCAW) covers about 1 million acres and is the world's largest waterway wilderness. *National Geographic Traveler* claims it's "one of 50 places everyone should visit in their lifetime." You must have a BWCAW permit to enter, and motorized or mechanized vehicles of any kind are prohibited (snowmobiles, mountain bikes, etc.). They also have a strict "leave no trace" policy. For more info on the BWCAW or to obtain a permit, log on to www.bwca.cc or call 877-444-6777.

2 Gunflint Lodge

143 South Gunflint Lake, Grand Marais; 800-328-3325 or 218-388-2294; www.gunflint.com. Lodge is located 43 miles northwest on Gunflint Trail (County 12).

There's no better way to "rough it" in the wilderness than to book a stay at the Gunflint Lodge. This third-generation, family-owned lodge features wood paneling and a stone fireplace. Their motto is: Arrive as a guest, and leave as a friend. A full friend, at that!

Feel like horseback riding through one of the most picturesque places on earth? Gunflint Lodge offers 1- and 2-hour trail rides through the Superior National Forest. Other riding packages include breakfast or dinner feasts prepared for you along the trail. The 24 cabins on Gunflint Lake range from 1–5 bedrooms. Some have indoor whirlpool baths and kitchens; some come equipped with a large outdoor whirlpool. All have living room fireplaces.

Gunflint Lodge specializes in "theme" vacations and retreats, such as mother and daughter weekends, lifestyle retreats, women's packages, fishing, canoeing, horseback riding, dogsledding, cross-country skiing and tree-to-tree zipline canopy tours. Fishing guides are available. On-staff naturalist. Pets allowed. Special rates for off-season. Check website for dates and prices.

3 Harley Trip to the Headwaters

Midwest Motorcycle, 215 Washington Avenue North; 888-237-5853; 612-338-5345; www.midwestmotorcycle.com. (Downtown Minneapolis in the heart of the Warehouse District.) Motorcycle endorsement must appear on your driver's license to rent.

Who among us has not wanted to feel wild and completely free? Get away from the grind by renting a weekend of freedom at **Midwest Motorcycle**. Straddle that powerful Harley and crank up the gas, because you're heading 200 miles north to the birthplace of something even more mighty than the beast between your legs: the Mississippi River in **Itasca State Park** (Minnesota's oldest state park). The main park entrance is 23 miles north of Park Rapids on Highway 71. The headwaters area is north and west of the east entrance off Park Drive.

It's at Itasca State Park that the Mississippi River begins her winding journey of more than 2,500 miles to the Gulf of Mexico. Stepping-stones cross over her humble beginnings. Spend some time hiking about 50 miles of trails through a virgin pine forest that boasts the state's tallest White Pine. The park also has two visitor centers, three gift shops, a 100-foot fire tower you can climb and year-round programs, including guided walks and boat tours. Bike, boat, canoe,

snowshoe and kayak rental available. Reserve lodging and camping well in advance by calling the State Park Reservation System at 866-85PARKS (866-857-2757) or www.stayatmnparks.com.

While in the area, eat at the historic **Douglas Lodge** (218-266-2122), located near the park's east entrance. Open Memorial Day weekend through the first Sunday in October. Decidedly Minnesotan, the menu includes such mainstays as wild rice soup and walleye. Wash down the meal with a nice bottle of wine—a Minnesota vintage, of course.

If you're looking for some evening entertainment, cruise on over to the **Woodtick Musical Theater** at the junction of Highways 34 & 64 in downtown Akeley (roughly a 40-mile drive). Enjoy two lively hours of country, gospel and bluegrass music and comedy routines. Mid-Jun through mid-Sep, W–Sa. Fee charged. Call 800-644-6892 for reservations or 218-652-4200 for information, or visit www.woodtick-theater.com.

Return to the Twin Cities via the **Great River Road** as it follows the Mississippi River between Itasca State Park and Little Falls. Travel the 200 miles through Bemidji, Grand Rapids, Aitkin and Brainerd. Watch for signs. NOTE: With all of the thick hardwood forests, the Great River Road is also a designated route for viewing fall color.

OPTION

If you have the time, head north of Itasca State Park to **Bemidji**. Have your picture taken next to huge statues of Paul Bunyan and Babe the Blue Ox, or any of the many sculptures along the waterfront. • **Lake Bemidji State Park** is 5 miles north of town on County 21, then 2 miles east on Highway 20, and worth your trip. You'll find naturalist programs, a boardwalk through a bog with insect-eating pitcher plants, miles of wooded trails and a swimming beach. The Showy Lady's Slipper (Minnesota's state flower) is in bloom from early June to early July. • The 32-mile **Scenic Byway County 39** runs between Blackduck and Cass Lake. **Star Island** (accessible by boat only) sits smack-dab in the middle of Cass Lake. The nearly 1,200-acre island is a mecca for Bald Eagles and boasts its own 195-acre lake, Lake Windigo—forming "a lake within an island within a lake." Say what?

4   Rock Climb & Sea Kayak

The University of Minnesota Duluth; 218-726-7128; www.umdrsop.org. Duluth is approximately 150 miles north of the Twin Cities on I-35. The actual site of the trips varies, so call ahead for locations.

Have you always wanted to learn how to kayak or rock climb? The University of Minnesota Duluth offers several options for learning these skills, including safety and rescue clinics. Take an introductory course at Split Rock Lighthouse State Park, kayaking the open waters of Lake Superior, or paddle next to anchored ocean freighters on Duluth Waterfront Tours. Rock climb on the North Shore and enjoy nature's beauty. Half- or full-day courses. Once you've mastered the courses, sign up for the University's adventure trips. There are several to choose from throughout the summer and they change from year to year. Skill level of trips varies from beginner to intermediate. Call or visit the University's website for schedule and pricing. A couple examples:

Mountain bike and rock climb in the Moab desert. Cycle through sandstone landscapes and stand on ancient rock spires.

Alpine climb in Rocky Mountain National Park. Attempt to take the summit at 14,225 feet.

5   Room to Roam Farm Vacations

Room to Roam, W656 Veraguth Drive, Fountain City, WI; 608-687-8575. Approximately 120 miles southeast of the Twin Cities.

As a guest at the Room to Roam, a registered Holstein dairy farm, you gather fresh eggs and feed the cows—all before breakfast! Afterward, watch farmer Jess work up the fields, bale some hay or harvest the crops. Learn what it's like to be a farmer in this challenging global economy or just pet the animals and enjoy the peace and quiet.

The furnished 3-bedroom, century-old, two-story farmhouse sits high on the bluffs overlooking the mighty Mississippi River. You'll have your own big maple tree in the front yard and a garden ripe for the picking in the back. There's a volleyball setup, Schwan's vanilla ice cream in the freezer, a firepit with a supply of wood, hayrides and plenty of time for eagle watching (so bring your binoculars). Rent by the night, weekend, week or longer. The house sleeps eight comfortably.

NOTE: This is not a bed and breakfast. You are responsible for your own meals. The farmhouse is separate from the owners' house.

6 Voyageurs National Park Houseboats

Voyageurs National Park: www.nps.gov/voya. Approximately 300 miles north of the Twin Cities, about a 5-hour drive.

Do you want to get away from it all? Then head to Voyageurs National Park. Located in the heart of the North Woods, Voyageurs is definitely in the "north country"; it shares a common boundary with Canada. More than 500 islands and over 30 lakes establishes it as the park with the most water. At 2.7 billion years old, Voyageurs' plentiful, gray-colored Canadian Shield is among the oldest rock in the world. Hunt, fish, canoe or pick blueberries to your heart's content. Visit old gold mines, a primitive sculpture garden or the historic Kettle Falls Hotel—reported as haunted! Hike trails to waterfalls, island hop or skinny-dip (if you're so inclined), because it's only you and miles of scenic, untamed nature.

There are four points of entry into Voyageurs besides International Falls: Crane Lake, Ash River, Lake Kabetogama and Rainy Lake. The following is a list of local houseboat rental firms:

Dougherty's Rainy Lake Houseboats, 2031 County Road 102, International Falls; 800-554-9188; www.rainylakehouseboats.com

Ebel's Voyageur Houseboats, 10326 Ash River Trail, Orr; 888-883-2357; www.ebels.com

Northernaire Houseboats, 2690 County 94, International Falls; 800-854-7958; www.northernairehouseboats.com

Voyagaire Lodge and Houseboats, 7576 Goldcoast Road, Crane Lake; 800-882-6287; www.voyagaire.com

Boats are furnished with kitchen equipment, dishes and bedding. Linens, towels and hot tubs available for rent. Some firms include fishing boats. Extensive instructions given to inexperienced boaters. Season: Mid-May to mid-Oct. Rates vary.

Before heading into the wilderness, make a stop at the **Vince Shute Wildlife Sanctuary** to learn a thing or two about Black Bears. From an observation deck, watch trained naturalists interpret bear behavior as it happens. But a word of caution—you enter the grounds at your own risk. Bears are wild animals and are not fenced in. Read the signs and follow all directions. The Sanctuary is also excellent for birding, so don't forget your binoculars! The Vince Shute Wildlife Sanctuary is 1 mile south of Orr on Pelican Lake. From Highway 53, turn west on County 23; drive 13 miles, sanctuary is on the right. Open Memorial Day–Labor Day, 5 p.m. until dusk. Closed Mondays and during heavy rainfall. Fee charged. For tour information, call 218-757-0172; www.americanbear.org. • The **Orr Bog Walk** is a half-mile jaunt with wildlife and pelicans galore! Boardwalk begins at the Information Center parking lot located just south of Orr on Highway 53. Call 218-757-3932 (Orr Tourist Information Center) for more information. Wheelchair accessible.

7 Wintergreen Dogsled Vacations

1101 Ring Rock Road, Ely; 877-SLEDFUN (877-753-3386) or 218-365-6022; www.dogsledding.com. Approximately 260 miles from the Twin Cities, about a 4-hour drive.

NOTE: Flying in? A few 45-minute trips are offered daily from the Twin Cities to Hibbing's full-service airport. Take the Ely Shuttle, which travels to Hibbing and Duluth airports, to the resort. Reserve ahead when you reserve your flight.

In 1986, Paul Schurke and Will Steger successfully completed an amazing 57-day journey to the North Pole. This launched new careers for them as best-selling authors and speakers with an award-winning television special. *Outside Magazine* named Paul the "Outdoorsman of the Year." This vacation gives you a chance to go exploring with real-life Arctic adventurer Paul Schurke. For the past couple of decades, Paul has conducted complete hands-on mushing tours from his Wintergreen Lodge on White Iron Lake.

Wintergreen provides gear, food and lodging. It also has the world's largest working kennel of Canadian Eskimo freight dogs. The dogs range from 60–80 pounds and can pull twice their weight. If you don't know what to wear, Paul's wife, Sue, can hook you up with fleece anoraks or pants or whatever you need to keep toasty warm. Sue Schurke is the owner of Wintergreen Design and sewed all the clothing for Paul's 1986 North Pole expedition, launching her extremely successful business from the kitchen table. Rent or buy the clothing at a special guest discount.

Wintergreen also has a French chef on staff. The Schurke family lives nearby on the grounds and often eats with the guests. Paul takes time to personally visit with the guests and share his Arctic adventures. Physical requirements vary for each trip, with a recommended age of 8 years or older. Group size is 6–8. Book in advance, as trips fill by November.

Schoolhouse on Gibbs Farm, St. Paul

This chapter has the whole family in mind with attractions geared to entertain and educate. You'll find some outings are seasonal, while others may be a bit more tailored to certain ages. Pick the ones that are right for your gang and have fun!

FAMILY DAY

ANCIENT CARVINGS
Jeffers Petroglyphs, *Comfrey*. 38
  Option: Blue Mounds State Park

CANNON RIVER TUBING
Welch Mill Canoeing and Tubing, *Welch* 38
  Option: Cannon Valley Trail

FARMING
Farmamerica, *Waseca* 39
  Options: Cabela's, Village of Yesteryear

JUST LIKE LAURA INGALLS WILDER
Sod House on the Prairie, *Sanborn*. 40

Walnut Grove—Laura Ingalls Wilder Museum 40

KIDS' MUSEUMS
Gibbs Farm, *St. Paul*. 41

Minnesota Children's Museum, *St. Paul* 41

Science Museum of Minnesota, *St. Paul*. 41

LIONS, TIGERS AND BEARS
Como Park Zoo, *St. Paul*. 42

Minnesota Zoo, *Apple Valley* 42

MALL OF AMERICA
Mall of America, *Bloomington* 42

MINNESOTA LEGENDS
Charles A. Lindbergh House, *Little Falls* 43

Minnesota Fishing Museum and Hall of Fame, *Little Falls* 43
  Option: Pine Grove Zoo

Paul Bunyan Trail, *Brainerd to Bemidji* 44

NATURE EXPERIENCE
Eagle Bluff Environmental Learning Center, *Lanesboro* 44
  Options: Avian Acres Wild Bird Supply, State DNR Fish Hatchery, Van Gundy's
  Elk Farm

PLAYTIME
Cascade Bay Water Park, *Eagan* 45

Grand Slam Sports, *Burnsville* 45

TEPEES AND FORTS

Alexander Ramsey Park, *Redwood Falls* 46

Birch Coulee Battlefield, *Morton* 46

Fort Ridgely, *Fairfax* 46

Lower Sioux Agency, *Redwood Falls* 47
Option: Morton Gneiss rocks

Upper Sioux Agency State Park, *Granite Falls* 47
Option: Minnesota's largest cottonwood

THE WILD NORTH

Big Lake Wilderness Lodge, *Ely* 47

International Wolf Center, *Ely* 48
Option: Dorothy Molter Cabin Museum

THINGS THAT FLY

National Eagle Center, *Wabasha* 49

Raptor Center, *St. Paul* 49

Valleyfair Amusement Park, *Shakopee* 49

Blue Mounds State Park

ANCIENT CARVINGS

1 Jeffers Petroglyphs

27160 County Road 2, Comfrey. Located 3 miles east of Highway 71 on County 10; then 1 mile south on County 2; 507-628-5591; sites/mnhs.org/historic-sites/jeffers-petroglyphs

The glacier-scarred bedrock contains thousands of ancient rock carvings known as petroglyphs. This is a sacred place, one that has been used by American Indian tribes for more than 7,000 years. Search the rock outcrops for carvings of bison, turtles, thunderbirds and human figures. The surrounding native prairie boasts cacti and other rare plants.

Visitor center with interactive activities, exhibits and video. Open Memorial Day–Labor Day, Su–M and W–Sa. Closed Saturdays in September. Wheelchair accessible. Fee charged.

NOTE: The Petroglyphs are easier to see during the morning, late afternoon or on a cloudy day.

OPTION

Although it's a bit out of the way, a trip to **Blue Mounds State Park** is well worth the added miles. The park takes its name from the cliff of Sioux quartzite that appeared blue to the settlers as they journeyed west. On the park's southern end is an unexplained 1,250-foot line of rocks that aligns with the sun on the first day of spring and fall. The northern end attracts visitors to a viewing platform for a look at a bison herd. Also has a campground, wildflower prairie with cacti and 7-foot-tall grasses. Park located in the southwest corner of Minnesota, 3 miles north of Luverne off Highway 75; 507-283-6050; www.dnr.state.mn.us/state_parks/blue_mounds/index.html.

CANNON RIVER TUBING

2 Welch Mill Canoeing and Tubing

Located in Welch on County 7 off of Highway 61; 651-388-9857 and 800-657-6760; www.welchmillcanoeandtube.com

Welch is a scene right out of a movie—literally. A big Hollywood production company filmed the motion picture *Here On Earth* in this picturesque village, using many of the locals as walk-ons. So look around, have an ice cream cone, then take a lazy ride down the Cannon River by canoe, kayak or inner tube. Ross Nelson of Welch Mill Canoeing and Tubing will happily provide you with a rental. If he's not too busy, he'll probably even shoot a few hoops with you. Rental price includes life jackets, paddles and shuttle service. If your bus driver happens to be an Irish storyteller named Bill, tell him his sister says hi! Open daily Memorial Day weekend–Labor Day weekend. Call for off-season hours. Five- or 12-mile trip. Cash or Minnesota check accepted; no credit/debit cards.

OPTION

A restful haven for weary bikers, Welch is the midway point on the 20-mile **Cannon Valley Trail**.

FARMING

3 Farmamerica

7367 360th Avenue. Located 80 miles south of the Twin Cities. Take I-35 south to Highway 14. Farmamerica is 4 miles west of Waseca on County 2; watch for signs; 507-835-2052; www.farmamerica.org

What kids don't want to grow up on a farm, and who can blame them? There are so many exciting things to see and do, from tending the animals to working in the garden or field. Unfortunately, the number of Minnesota family farms is dwindling, but you can still get a hands-on farming experience by visiting Farmamerica—the state's agricultural interpretive center. A self-guided walking tour takes you through 150 years of farming, including an 1850s settlement, a 1930s farm and the latest farming practices. Understand how and why agriculture evolved from subsistence farming in the 1800s to the efficient food production of today.

Every weekend is special at Farmamerica. Follow the growing season and watch animals as they grow. On-site demonstrations include sheep shearing, shingle making, hay baling, small grain harvest, meat smoking and weaving on a century-old loom. There are also draft horses, antique tractors, threshing and the latest GPS-guided equipment. Gift shop and silo lookout, slide show, quilt show and displays. Open Memorial Day–Labor Day. Wheelchair accessible. Fee charged.

OPTION

Cabela's is the largest hunting, fishing and outdoor retail center in the Midwest and only 20 miles east of Farmamerica on I-35 in Owatonna (take exit 45). The store features a 35-foot-tall mountain with mounted animals in realistic settings, 54,000 gallons of freshwater aquariums, interactive demonstration

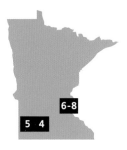

areas and a restaurant that serves elk sandwiches. Famous shoppers to Cabela's include Garth Brooks, Trisha Yearwood and Walter Payton. Open daily; 507-451-4545; www.cabelas. com. Wheelchair accessible. • The **Village of Yesteryear** is at 1448 Austin Road, next to the Owatonna fairgrounds. A unique boardwalk meanders through the 19-building village, providing a look at life during the turn of the twentieth century. May–Sep. Closed Mondays. Fee charged; 507-451-1420; www.steelehistorymuseum.org/index.php/village-yesteryear.

JUST LIKE LAURA INGALLS WILDER

These attractions visit the home territory of beloved author Laura Ingalls Wilder. It's also your chance to be a real pioneer family. Show your youngsters what it was like to live on the prairie without electricity or indoor plumbing.

4 Sod House on the Prairie

12598 Magnolia Avenue, Sanborn; 507-723-5138; www.sodhouse.org

To reach the authentic 1880 sod house replica, just follow a trail through 8-foot-tall prairie grass. The house has 2-foot-thick walls and a grass roof. Inside, you'll find whitewashed walls, oil lamps for light, two double beds, a fainting couch, a wood-burning stove, a wash pitcher and bowl, prairie clothes to dress up in and—oh, yes—a backyard outhouse! Explore the trapper's cabin complete with furs, traps and Indian artifacts. Open spring, summer and fall. Fee charged. Bring cash—no credit cards.

5 Walnut Grove—Laura Ingalls Wilder Museum

Laura Ingalls Wilder Museum; 800-528-7280; www.walnutgrove.org

In 1874, seven-year-old Laura Ingalls Wilder and her family traveled from Wisconsin's Big Woods to Walnut Grove, Minnesota, settling on the banks of Plum Creek. The community preserves Laura's past and celebrates with an annual festival in her honor. Visit the Laura Ingalls Wilder Museum located at 330 8th Street. Here you'll see "Grandma's

House" among the four buildings at the main museum site. The Ingalls' homestead site is 1½ miles north of the museum. Apr–Oct, open daily. Fee charged. Gift store at the museum is open year-round.

KIDS' MUSEUMS

Here are a few museums that have nothing to do with boring and everything to do with fun. Entertaining and educational, your kids won't be the only ones having a good time!

6 Gibbs Farm

2097 West Larpenteur Avenue, St. Paul; 651-646-8629; www.rchs.com/gbbsfm2.htm

At the Gibbs Farm, costumed interpreters demonstrate what life was like during the nineteenth century. Family-friendly site that offers several day camps and seasonal programs. Open Sa–Su, Memorial weekend–Oct. Wheelchair accessible. Fee charged. Children under age 1 are free.

7 Minnesota Children's Museum

10 West 7th Street (7th and Wabasha), St. Paul; 651-225-6000; www.mcm.org

One of the state's coolest places to explore, the Minnesota Children's Museum offers lots of imaginative and colorful hands-on activities. Operate a crane or don an ant costume and crawl through an anthill maze. The only trouble is, this museum is so much fun that the adults want a turn at the exhibits, too! Open daily. Wheelchair accessible. Fee charged; kids under 1 are free.

8 Science Museum of Minnesota

120 West Kellogg Boulevard (across from the RiverCentre), St. Paul; 651-221-9444; www.smm.org

The Science Museum of Minnesota is home to a famous, long-dead resident—the mummy. Kids love mummies almost as much as they love dinosaurs. Luckily, the museum has both! Interactive displays allow you to control the choppers on a ferocious *T. rex*, make tornadoes, wander the bloodstream superhighway or view your own cells. Climb aboard a real towboat or enjoy a movie in the Omnitheater. Head outdoors to the Big Back Yard for a challenging game of minigolf. The 9-hole course is a twisting river of scientific questions about water patterns and erosion. Afterward, take a walk through a prairie grass maze and enjoy the many other activities found in the Big Back Yard. Open daily. Closed Mondays, mid-Sep to mid-Dec. Gift shop, two restaurants. Wheelchair accessible. Fee charged.

12-13

9-11

LIONS, TIGERS AND BEARS

9 Como Park Zoo

1225 Estabrook Drive, St. Paul. 24-hour Information: 651-487-8200; Customer Service: 651-487-8201; www.comozooconservatory.org

A St. Paul landmark since 1897, the Como Zoo boasts a wide variety of animals, including everything from lions, tigers, and giraffes to critters like bison and wolves that are found in our neck of the woods. With dining options, a great gift shop, and the famous "Sparky the Seal" show, which has been wowing fans since its inception in 1956, a trip to the zoo is the perfect way to spend a day. Check the website for information on special events, programs and more.

10 Minnesota Zoo

13000 Zoo Boulevard, Apple Valley; 800-366-7811 or 952-431-9200; www.mnzoo.com

See thousands of animals representing more than 500 species from five continents in naturalistic settings, including Amur tigers, Chinese takins, South African penguins, wolverines and many other rare and endangered species. The zoo features miles of outdoor trails and the largest indoor interconnected zoo exhibits in the country. Take in an animal show, or see a movie at the IMAX Theatre. Learn about farm animals at the Wells Fargo Family Farm. Concessions; wheelchair accessible (electric wheelchairs available). Fee charged for zoo and parking. Separate fee for IMAX Theatre (free parking for IMAX-only visits).

MALL OF AMERICA

11 Mall of America

Located at the junction of I-494 and Highway 77 (Cedar Avenue South) in Bloomington; 952-883-8800; www.mallofamerica.com

With over 40 million guests annually, MOA is one of the United States' most-visited destinations. And why not? There's so much to do in this "city within a city." Of course there's the shopping with more than 520 stores for your perusal, but there's also a 14-screen movie theatre, comedy club, restaurants, and nightclubs. Say your "I do's" in the Chapel of Love where more than 7,000 weddings have been performed.

For the kids, you'll find Nickelodeon Universe—a 7-acre amusement park with lots of exciting rides, an 18-hole miniature golf course, and roaming Nickelodeon characters the kids will have fun meeting. Or take the kids to GRUB—a fun place full of pizza, Dippin' Dots, ICEE Mix It Up and more. And you won't want to miss the SEA LIFE Minnesota Aquarium—the world's largest underground aquarium and home to more than 10,000 ocean species including sharks, giant green sea turtles, octopi, stingrays, sea horses, and much more. The adventurous types can scuba dive with the sharks, feed them, or even throw a slumber party in the aquarium. The aquarium features a 300-foot ocean tunnel, 30 display tanks, and hands-on activities.

MINNESOTA LEGENDS

Brainerd is approximately 150 miles north of the Twin Cities. Take Highway 10 to Highway 371 into Brainerd; 800-450-2838 or 218-829-2838; www.explorebrainerdlakes.com.

12 Charles A. Lindbergh House

1620 Lindbergh Drive South, Little Falls (2 miles south of town); 320-616-5421; www.mnhs.org/lindbergh

Charles A. Lindbergh Jr., the first person to fly across the Atlantic Ocean alone, spent his boyhood summers at this cottage on the Mississippi River. The 1906 house contains original furnishings and family heirlooms. History center features a gift shop, family exhibits, a 17-minute documentary, as well as some of Lindbergh's inventions and aviation accomplishments. Open daily Memorial Day–Labor Day, Th–Su. Wheelchair accessible. Fee charged.

13 Minnesota Fishing Museum and Hall of Fame

304 West Broadway (Highway 27), Little Falls; 320-616-2011; www.mnfishingmuseum.com

You can't take the kids on a "legends" trip without stopping in at the Minnesota Fishing Museum for a look at some fish legends. The museum's showrooms boast a live aquarium, thousands of decoys, lures, boats, motors, as well as a 1920s fishing and hunting cabin and several state record fish replicas. The museum is wheelchair accessible and open year-round. Fee charged, but free for children ages 5 and under.

14

16-17

15

OPTION

While you're in Little Falls, visit the **Pine Grove Zoo**. Walk through their deer pen. See bison, tigers and elk. Children's playground. Located at 1200 West Broadway (Highway 27); 320-616-5595; www.pinegrovezoo.com. Open mid-Apr to mid-Oct, daily. Fee charged.

14 Paul Bunyan Trail

Brainerd to Bemidji; www.paulbunyantrail.com

One of Minnesota's most famous and gigantic citizens is Paul Bunyan. Paul's footprints, along with those of his sidekick Babe the Blue Ox, created the state's more than 10,000 lakes . . . or so the legend goes.

Hike, bike, in-line skate or snowmobile the 120-mile paved Paul Bunyan Trail from Brainerd to Bemidji. Very scenic with 14 towns, 21 lakes, 4 rivers and countless streams. For more information, contact the Brainerd Lakes Area Chamber of Commerce or log on to the Paul Bunyan Trail website, where you can play tic-tac-toe with Paul and Babe or read more about their legendary antics.

NOTE: Road and mountain bikes, in-line skates, and skis available for rent at Easy Riders Bicycle and Sportshop, 415 Washington Street, Brainerd; 218-829-5516; easyridersbikes.com. Shuttle service available.

NATURE EXPERIENCE

15 Eagle Bluff Environmental Learning Center

28097 Goodview Drive, Lanesboro; 507-467-2437; www.eagle-bluff.org

Nestled amid the hardwood forests and river bluffs of southeast Minnesota, Eagle Bluff Environmental Learning Center strives to provide inspiring environmental education experiences, which connect people of all ages to each other and the natural world. Whether you are looking for a memorable educational field trip, a unique family outdoor adventure or an inspiring place to hold your retreat, there is learning and discovery to be had at Eagle Bluff! Eagle Bluff offers scheduled public events, such as a Maple Syrup Fest,

Summer High Ropes Challenge, Skills School Classes, the Dinner on the Bluff Series, Candlelight Snowshoe trips, and more. If you can't join them for one of their scheduled events, stop by the Schroeder Visitor's Center, walk or ski one of their trails or check out the public geocaching course.

OPTION

Less than 10 miles from Eagle Bluff, you'll find **Avian Acres Wild Bird Supply**. Located 1.5 miles southwest of Lanesboro off County Road 8 (32637 Grit Road); follow the signs; 507-467-2996. Avian Acres specializes in wild bird supplies and attracting backyard birds. Relax in their rural setting while enjoying the antics of colorful songbirds. Expert advice, books, gifts, and more. Open year-round; www.avianacres. com • The **State DNR Fish Hatchery**, located a few miles south of Lanesboro, produces more trout per year than any other state hatchery. Free 17-minute video, self-guided tour and interpretive trail. Large group guided tours are available, call ahead; dnr.state.mn.us/areas/fisheries/lanesboro-hatchery/index.htm • **Van Gundy's Elk Farm** is 3 miles north of Houston on Highway 76 (less than 30 miles from Eagle Bluff). Herd has over 50 elk. Learn what elk eat, what their mannerisms are and how to care for them, and see the spring calves. Call ahead; 507-896-2380.

PLAYTIME
16 Cascade Bay Water Park

1360 Civic Center Drive, Eagan; 651-675-5577; www.cascadebay.com

There's a saying in Minnesota: "It's not the heat, it's the humidity." If your family starts feeling the heat, take them to Cascade Bay Water Park. Shoot down Twin Falls or brave the Typhoon and Hurricane water slides. Feeling a bit more mellow? Then take a relaxing float on an inner tube in the Lazy River. The little ones have their own sprays, spouts and shipwreck slide. Open Jun–Labor Day weekend. Check website for days and hours. Concessions. Fee charged.

17 Grand Slam Sports

12425 River Ridge Boulevard, Burnsville; 952-224-0413; www.grandslammn.com

Go to Grand Slam Sports for a spirited game of laser tag or a challenging round of mini-golf. Watch your kids squeal with delight as they ram and dodge in bumper cars. Over 30,000 square feet boasts batting cages, video arcade, snack bar and more for the whole family. Open daily.

18-22

23

TEPEES AND FORTS

18 Alexander Ramsey Park

Located on the northwest end of Redwood Falls, turn north on Lincoln Street and follow signs. Redwood Falls Community Center: 507-644-2333; www.redwoodareacommunitycenter.com

Redwood Falls is southeast of the Upper Sioux Agency on Highway 71 and home to the state's largest municipal park, Alexander Ramsey Park, affectionately termed "The Little Yellowstone of Minnesota." It contains a zoo with bison, elk and peacocks, waterfalls, a DNR trout stream, paved hiking trails with very cool footbridges, a ball diamond, a children's play area, picnic grounds and a campground. Free.

19 Birch Coulee Battlefield

3 miles north of Morton, 32469 County 2; 800-657-3773; sites.mnhs.org/historic-sites/birch-coulee-battlefield

Soldiers from nearby Fort Ridgely, on a mission to bury dead civilians caught in the U.S.-Dakota War of 1862, found themselves in one of the hardest-fought battles of the conflict. Visitors can tour the self-guided trails where markers explain the battle from Dakota and U.S. soldiers' perspectives. The site is listed on the National Register of Historic Places. May–Oct, dawn until dusk. Free.

20 Fort Ridgely

7 miles south of Fairfax on Highway 4; 507-508-2848; sites.mnhs.org/historic-sites/fort-ridgely

Built in 1853, Fort Ridgely was intended as a police station for keeping the peace between new settlers and the Dakota. Learn about the daily lives of the people who lived and worked in this Civil War-era military fort. Try on prairie clothing, soldiers' wool uniforms and handle a musket. Lots of hands-on exhibits. Open Memorial Day weekend–Oct. Check website for days and hours. Minnesota State Park permit required.

21 Lower Sioux Agency

Interpretive center located 9 miles east of Redwood Falls, 32469 County 2; 507-697-6321; sites.mnhs.org/historic-sites/lower-sioux-agency

At the history center, learn about the Agency's purpose, and the Dakota story before, during and after the U.S.-Dakota War of 1862. Open May–Labor Day. Wheelchair accessible. Fee charged.

NOTE: Outcrops of rock visible from the highway near the town of Morton—called **Morton Gneiss**—are 3.5 billion years old. These swirled, multicolored rocks are gray, red and black and are among the oldest in the world!

22 Upper Sioux Agency State Park

State Highway 67 (8 miles southeast of Granite Falls); 866-857-2757 (reservations); www.dnr.state.mn.us/state_parks/upper_sioux_agency/index.html

Have you ever wanted to camp in a teepee? Head to Upper Sioux Agency State Park. The Minnesota and Yellow Medicine Rivers provide spectacular fishing, hiking and birding. Spot Red-tailed Hawks, pelicans, Blue Herons and Belted Kingfishers. The park features a children's play area, horseshoe pits, volleyball courts and an equestrian camp. Only two tepees, so reserve early. Regular camping also offered. Fee charged.

OPTION

See **Minnesota's largest cottonwood**! Growing since 1860, the tree has a trunk 30 feet in circumference. To get there, go 8 miles northwest of Montevideo on Highway 59; turn left on Highway 13 for 2.2 miles, then right 1 mile on County 32. Right side of road; look for small sign.

THE WILD NORTH

Ely is approximately 255 miles north of the Twin Cities. Take I-35 north toward Duluth, then turn onto Highway 33, which connects with Highway 53. Follow 53 north to Highway 169 east into Ely. Visit Ely's Chamber of Commerce at www.ely.org.

23 Big Lake Wilderness Lodge

3012 Echo Trail, Ely; 800-446-9080 or 218-365-2125; www.biglakelodge.com

Located on a peninsula at an entry point for the BWCAW, the lodge is a great place to bring the kids. Not only do you get to stay in a roomy log cabin with a spectacular view of a lake filled with prize walleyes, but there are also nature hikes, berry picking, craft classes, and family movie nights. Bring your mountain bike and ride the

rugged trails or make use of the canoes, kayaks and paddleboats the lodge provides. Bird watchers delight in the wide variety of species. The lodge store carries grocery staples, bait and souvenirs. Lounge, sauna. Some cabins are wheelchair accessible.

24 International Wolf Center

1396 Highway 169, Ely; 800-ELY-WOLF (800-359-9653) or 218-365-4695; www.wolf.org. Located at the far end of town.

Don't miss the International Wolf Center on your trip up north! The center features a live ambassador wolf pack that you can view from the center's beautiful amphitheater, and it's also home to the Wolves and Humans exhibit designed by the Science Museum of Minnesota. And there's so much more; the daily schedule includes programs like Pup to Predator, Jr., Wolf Detective, and The Mighty Miserable Moose.

For younger kids, there is the Little Wolf den where they will crawl into the den to hear the whimpering of wolf pups, and do lots of fun hands-on activities and games! The International Wolf Center is open May through October; days and hours vary by month. For admission prices and more information, visit www.wolf.org.

OPTION

Visit the **Dorothy Molter Cabin Museum** located on Highway 169 (near the International Wolf Center). Molter was the last resident of the BWCAW. Each year as many as 6,000 visitors from all over the world stopped by her cabin for a bottle of her homemade root beer. After her death in 1986, Molter's homestead was dismantled and transported to Ely where volunteers painstakingly restored two of the cabins. Gift shop, interpretive center, bird-feeding area and nature trail. Check website for days and hours; 218-365-4451; www.rootbeerlady.com. The cabins are wheelchair accessible; the trail is not. Fee charged.

THINGS THAT FLY

Whether it's birds or a thrill ride, kids love things that fly. Try one of these to satisfy your children's (or your) dreams of flight.

25 National Eagle Center

50 Pembroke Avenue, Box 242, Wabasha; 877-332-4537 or 651-565-4989; www.nationaleaglecenter.org

Did you know that an eagle's average flight speed is 30 mph, with a dive speed around 100 mph? Did you know that an eagle's nest weighs hundreds of pounds? Learn all about these fascinating birds of prey at the beautiful and spacious National Eagle Center. Observation decks with spotting scopes are also available. Trained guides are on hand to answer your questions on weekends during the "eagle season" (Nov–Mar). Visit Angel, Columbia, Donald and Was'aka—the Center's resident educational eagles—or explore the newest interactive exhibit "Discover the Refuge!," which introduces visitors to the Upper Mississippi River National Fish & Wildlife Refuge. The Center is open daily, year-round. Fee charged.

26 Raptor Center

1920 Fitch Avenue, St. Paul (on the University of Minnesota campus); 612-624-4745; www.theraptorcenter.org

See Great Horned Owls, Red-tailed Hawks, eagles and many more birds of prey at the world-renowned Raptor Center. Learn interesting facts about the birds from on-staff naturalists. The center functions as a hospital for injured birds. Once recovered, birds are released back into the wild. Open year-round. Wheelchair accessible. Fee charged for tours.

27 Valleyfair Amusement Park

1 Valleyfair Drive, Shakopee; 952-445-6500; www.valleyfair.com

Now it's your turn to fly at Valleyfair! The park has more than 75 rides, attractions and live entertainment, from 8 soaring roller coasters and 90-foot waterslides to the family-friendly Route 76, Planet Snoopy and Soak City Waterpark, included in the admission price. Concessions. Wheelchair accessible. Check website for days and hours.

Marjorie McNeely Conservatory

More people than ever before list gardening as their #1 hobby. This chapter showcases some of the most spectacular gardens nurtured in Minnesota. So even if you don't care to keep a garden yourself, you can still enjoy the fruits of someone else's labors.

GARDEN TOURS

A SERENE FEAST FOR THE SOUL
Caponi Art Park, *Eagan* 52

Minnesota Landscape Arboretum, *Chanhassen*. 52

METRO AREA GARDENS
Eloise Butler Wildflower Garden & Bird Sanctuary, *Minneapolis* . . . 53

Lyndale Rose Garden, *Minneapolis* 53
Option: Thomas Sadler Roberts Bird Sanctuary

Marjorie McNeely Conservatory, *St. Paul* 53

Minneapolis Sculpture Garden, *Minneapolis* 54
Option: Walker Art Center

Noerenberg Memorial Gardens, *Orono* 55

SOUTHERN MINNESOTA GARDENS
Mayo Park & Arboretum, *Le Sueur*. 55
Option: W. W. Mayo House

Linnaeus Arboretum & Sculpture Garden, *St. Peter* 55

August Schell Brewery, *New Ulm* 56

Gilfillan Estate, *Redwood Falls*. 56
Option: Redwood County Museum

ST. CLOUD GARDENS
Clemens Rose Gardens. 57

Munsinger Gardens. 57
Option: Stearns History Museum

A SERENE FEAST FOR THE SOUL

There's nothing like a garden to help you unplug, unwind and reconnect with what really matters in your life.

1 Caponi Art Park

1220 Diffley Road, Eagan; 651-454-9412; www.caponiartpark.org

Put your Chi in harmony by exploring Caponi Art Park. This is an outdoor sculpture garden designed within an oak landscape, as well as nature trails and a theater program. Self-guided tours are available in the summer months. Free. Arranged tours available.

2 Minnesota Landscape Arboretum

3675 Arboretum Drive, Chanhassen; 952-443-1400. www.arboretum.umn.edu

The Minnesota Landscape Arboretum encompasses over 1200 acres with 46 display areas and specialty gardens. With more than 5,000 plant species and 45 plant collections, the Arboretum is the premiere garden and plant research facility in the Midwest and is part of the University of Minnesota.

Thousands of spring tulips, lilacs, crabapple blossoms and wildflowers explode every spring, bringing unimaginable color and scents, birds and blooms and myriad opportunities to explore nature. The Japanese garden, a hosta glade, herb and wildflower gardens and dazzling annual and perennial beds beckon in summer. Three rose gardens, world-class sculptures, fountains and extraordinary outdoor rooms showcase the plant, shrub and tree collections. The Three-Mile Drive allows visitors to walk or drive through the grounds from spring through fall. The new Dog Commons is the perfect place to hike with furry friends.

Fall activities include 30 varieties of apples grown on the grounds (including Honey Crisp and Haralson, two of many U of M introductions), harvest festivals, scarecrow building and a magnificent show of autumn color. Colder seasons allow cross-country skiing and snowshoeing on 16 miles of picturesque trails. Indoors, find delicious, homemade foods at our certified green café, including organic Arboretum produce and scrumptious bakery items. The Andersen Horticultural Library houses amazing rare books available for research and its own exhibits. View rotating shows in the two art galleries and the Meyer-Deats Conservatory, where exotic and tropical plants reside.

The gift shop showcases nature-inspired jewelry, children's gifts and books, gardening merchandise, home décor and items for friends and family. Fee for ages 13 and up (free for members). Third M each month is free from noon to 6 p.m. Open daily except Christmas and Thanksgiving.

METRO AREA GARDENS

3 Eloise Butler Wildflower Garden & Bird Sanctuary

Located off Wirth Parkway, south of Highway 55; 612-370-4903; www.minneapolisparks.org

The Eloise Butler Wildflower Garden is thought to be the oldest public wildflower garden in the U.S. Founded in 1907, botanist Eloise Butler understood the importance of conservation long before it became a cool thing to do. Hike the garden's 14 acres of trails through shady woodlands, bogs and prairies. Interpretive center open daily, Apr–Oct. Free. Guided tours and special programs offered weekends—fee may be charged.

4 Lyndale Rose Garden

4125 East Lake Harriet Parkway, Minneapolis; 612-230-6400; www.minneapolisparks.org

Also established in 1907, the Lyndale Rose Garden is the second-oldest public rose garden in the country. Expansive rose gardens, exotic and native trees, perennials and fountains. Open daily.

OPTION

Bring your binoculars because next to the gardens are is the **Thomas Sadler Roberts Bird Sanctuary**; it boasts 31 acres overall, with 13 acres of wetlands and woods.

5 Marjorie McNeely Conservatory

Located between Hamline and Lexington Avenues on Midway Boulevard in St. Paul; 651-487-8200; www.comozooconservatory.org

With just one foot inside the glass-enclosed Marjorie McNeely Conservatory you'll swear you're deep inside a jungle paradise surrounded by calling birds and flowing water. The humidity hangs

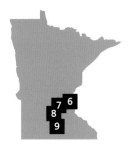

thick on even the most frigid of Minnesota days, and color abounds from exotic orange-blue birds of paradise and sassy hot-pink orchids. Banana trees, hanging vines, wispy ferns, tropical fish, a sunken garden and so much more. The only thing missing is Tarzan! Open daily. Wheelchair accessible. Free, donation suggested.

NOTE: The adjoining Como Park Zoo is free (donation suggested) and open daily.

6 Minneapolis Sculpture Garden

Located on Vineland Place across from the Guthrie Theater and the Walker Art Center, Minneapolis; 612-375-7600; www.walkerart.org/garden

The newly renovated Minneapolis Sculpture garden reopens in summer of 2017, when the vision for the 19-acre Walker Art Center and Minneapolis Sculpture Garden campus is realized. When the Minneapolis Sculpture Garden opens within the redeveloped Walker Art Center campus in June 2017, visitors will see the return of favorite artworks, such as the Twin Cities' landmark *Spoonbridge and Cherry* Sculpture, as well as the addition of 16 new pieces, from bold new works sure to become icons to new creations by contemporary artists from Minnesota and around the world. Open daily (after June 2017), 6 a.m.–midnight. Free.

OPTION

The **Walker Art Center** will remain open during construction of the campus, with a new entry pavilion and restaurant opening in November 2016. The Walker is one of the country's leading contemporary art museums and houses a permanent collection of paintings, photographs and sculptures. The facility features galleries filled with modern and contemporary art, films, performances, a restaurant and outdoor terraces with spectacular views. Closed Mondays. Wheelchair accessible. Fee charged, but free for visitors age 18 and under.

7 Noerenberg Memorial Gardens

2840 North Shore Drive, Orono; 763-559-6700; www.threeriversparkdistrict.org

Located near Lake Minnetonka's Crystal Bay in Orono, the Noerenberg Gardens feature an amazing collection of daylilies and azaleas, as well as a vast and vibrant rainbow of annuals and perennials. Open daily, May 1 through mid-Oct. Free.

SOUTHERN MINNESOTA GARDENS

8 Mayo Park & Arboretum

Le Sueur. On the north end of town on County 28.

Some years ago, the mother and daughter team behind the greeting card company "it takes two" decided to build their corporate headquarters in Le Sueur for one simple reason: the flower gardens. The Mayo Park and Arboretum features rose beds, a white garden, herbs, over 20 hosta varieties, bulbs and perennials. Free.

OPTION

While you're in town, tour the **W. W. Mayo House**. 118 North Main Street; 507-665-3250; mayohouse.org. Costumed interpreters guide you through the 1859 home of Mayo Clinic founder W. W. Mayo. The doctor set up his first medical practice in a room upstairs. After the good doctor left for Rochester, the Cosgroves—founders of the Green Giant Company—moved into the house in 1874. Check website for days and hours. Fee charged. Free for children age 5 and under.

9 Linnaeus Arboretum & Sculpture Garden

St. Peter, on the grounds of Gustavus Adolphus College. Main entrance is on College Avenue; 507-933-6181; www.gustavus.edu/arboretum

The Linnaeus Arboretum has areas representing the three major natural ecosystems found in Minnesota: coniferous forests, deciduous woodlands and prairies. A fourth area, cultivated gardens and trees from other regions, surrounds the Melva Lind Interpretive Center. Lilac walk, bluebird trail, 1866 Swedish pioneer cabin, exhibits and programs. Free.

10 August Schell Brewery

New Ulm. Go south on Broadway, then turn west on 18th Street; follow signs; 800-770-5020 or 507-354-5528; www.schellsbrewery.com

A brewery in the gardens chapter? No, this is not a joke. Schell's is the second-oldest family-owned brewery in the nation and they do offer a tour of the operation for a small fee, but the gorgeous gardens with peacocks strutting about are open to the public for free. Arbors, roses, annual and perennial beds. Also a deer park, museum and gift shop.

11 Gilfillan Estate

Located on Highway 67 between Redwood Falls and Morgan; 507-249-2210; redwoodcountyhistoricalsociety.com/gilfillan-estate

The Gilfillan Estate is a restored 1882 farm with a beautiful yard and flower gardens. The estate includes the home's original furniture, a summer kitchen, antique farm machinery and farm buildings. Guided tours. Open Jun–Labor Day, Sa–Su. Small fee charged.

OPTION

Since you're so close, the **Redwood County Museum** is worth a visit. Located west of Redwood Falls on Highway 19, the museum occupies what was once a Poor Farm. Thirty rooms display local history and period furnishings. Also on the grounds is a country schoolhouse and a one-cell jail from 1865. Open May–Sep, Th–Su; 507-641-3329; redwoodcountyhistoricalsociety.com/museum.

ST. CLOUD GARDENS

12 Clemens Rose Gardens

1301 Killian Boulevard, St. Cloud; 320-257-5959;
www.munsingerclemens.com

Parallel to the Munsinger Gardens, Bill Clemens donated the beautiful Clemens Rose Gardens to the city of St. Cloud as a dedication to his wife, Virginia. Suffering from multiple sclerosis, Mrs. Clemens needed only look out her window to gaze at the more than 1,200 rosebushes directly across the street. Considered to be one of the largest public rose gardens in the state, the Clemens Rose Gardens consist of six connecting formal gardens. Open daily: Sunrise–sunset. Free.

13 Munsinger Gardens

1515 Riverside Drive Southeast, St. Cloud; 320-257-5959;
www.munsingerclemens.com

Located on the scenic banks of the Mississippi River, the Munsinger Gardens came to life in 1915 as part of a park. The gardens now boast huge shade trees, a lily pond with fountain, a gazebo, benches to rest upon and a pair of peacocks. Open daily: Sunrise–sunset. Free.

OPTION

The **Stearns History Museum** is a great place to learn about Central Minnesota's history. Two floors of spectacular exhibits include a life-size replica of a granite quarry, the controversial 1919 Pan Automobile, and a century-old dairy setup. The large Research Center specializes in genealogical information from Luxembourg and Germany. It also houses tons of intriguing information about the granite and dairy industries, sports, and architecture. Kids have a blast in the Children's Gallery. The Stearns History Museum has a gift store, movies, gardens, and hiking trails. They are at 235 South 33rd Avenue, St. Cloud; 866-253-8424 or 320-253-8424; www.stearns-museum.org. Open daily, year-round. Fee charged; children age 4 and under are free.

GARDEN TOURS

Niagara Cave

Is there anything more exciting than exploring a cave? It's cold, it's wet, it's dark and it's a place where our imaginations are free to run wild! In a cave, we, too, can be Ali Baba hunting for treasures or the heroic Batman fighting off thugs.

This chapter explores some very interesting Minnesota caves; one has a waterfall and another boasts a beautiful lake. There's even a cave with a fireplace!

GEOLOGY & CAVE TOURS

THE MESABI IRON RANGE

Taconite State Trail: Grand Rapids 60
Options: Judy Garland Children's Museum, Forest History Center, Blandin Paper Mill

Hill Annex Mine State Park: Calumet 61

Hull Rust Mahoning Mine: Hibbing 61
Options: North Hibbing, Greyhound Bus Museum, Hibbing Historical Society Museum, Hibbing Public Library—Bob Dylan exhibit

Minnesota Discovery Center: Chisholm 62
Options: Hibbing Taconite Company Mine Tour, Minnesota Museum of Mining

USS Minntac: Mountain Iron 63

Leonidas Overlook: Eveleth 63
Options: United States Hockey Hall of Fame Museum, World's Largest Free-standing Hockey Stick

Iron Trail: Biwabik 63
Option: Eli Wirtanen Finnish Farmstead

Longyear Drill Site: Hoyt Lakes 64

Lake Vermilion-Soudan Underground Mine State Park: Soudan . . 64

SOUTHEASTERN MINNESOTA'S BLUFF COUNTRY

Mystery Cave, *Preston* 65
Options: Forestville/Mystery Cave State Park, Historic Forestville, Spring Valley: Methodist Church from "Little House"

Niagara Cave, *Harmony* 65
Options: Amish tours, Amish Buggy Byway

TWIN CITIES CAVES

Battle Creek Park, *Maplewood* 66

Wabasha Street Caves, *St. Paul* 66
Options: Gangster tours, Mississippi River rides

WESTERN WISCONSIN'S PIERCE COUNTY

Crystal Cave, *Spring Valley, WI* 67

Eau Galle Dam, *Spring Valley, WI* 67
Option: Elmwood, WI, UFO capital of the world

Nugget Lake County Park, *Plum City, WI* 68

THE MESABI IRON RANGE

From the Twin Cities, take Highway 169 approximately 175 miles north to the Mesabi Iron Range Tourism Bureau; 800-777-8497; www.ironrange.org.

The official Mesabi Iron Range consists of Hibbing and those towns east to Hoyt Lakes. However, this section covers more than the Iron Range and includes an area 100 miles north from Grand Rapids to Soudan. No caves on this venture, but lots of fascinating mining operations and geology stuff.

NOTE: The aurora borealis (northern lights) occur regularly in this region, creating a rainbow of colors and shapes against the night sky. They are especially active during the spring and fall.

1 Taconite State Trail: Grand Rapids

Grand Rapids Chamber of Commerce; 800-472-6366; www.grandmn.com or www.dnr.state.mn.us/state_trails/taconite/index.html

The 165-mile Taconite State Trail (paved for the first 6 miles outside of Grand Rapids) provides a great view of old mining operations. It's perfect for bikers, hikers, horseback riders and snowmobilers.

OPTION

Grand Rapids is the birthplace of singer/actress Judy Garland. Skip along the yellow brick sidewalk downtown before touring the plain, two-story white house (has some original furniture) that was Judy's childhood home. Also visit the **Judy Garland Children's Museum** located at 2727 Pokegama Avenue South. The museum houses props from the movie *The Wizard of Oz*. Check website for days and hours; 800-664-5839; www.judygarlandmuseum.com. Fee charged. • A visit to the **Forest History Center** (2609 County 76) is a trip back into the early 1900s. Learn what life was like for loggers through costumed interpreters. Also an interpretive center with movies and exhibits. Open daily. Fee charged; sites.mnhs.org/historic-sites/forest-history-center. • Learn how wood becomes paper at the **Blandin Paper Mill**, 122 Northwest 3rd Street (alongside the Mississippi River); 45- minute tour for ages 12 and up.

Must wear closed-toe shoes. Open Jun–Aug, W–F. For more info call 218-327-6682. Free.

2 Hill Annex Mine State Park: Calumet

Calumet is roughly 14 miles northeast of Grand Rapids on Highway 169. Hill Annex Mine State Park is north of Calumet on Highway 169; 218-247-7215; www.dnr.state.mn.us/state_parks/hill_annex_mine

The Hill Annex Mine State Park was a thriving, open-pit iron ore mine until its closure in 1978. Take the 90-minute bus tour 500 feet down into the heart of the pit. Tour winds past huge mining machinery and company buildings. Special fossil hunting tours available. Tours run F–Sa, Memorial Day weekend–Labor Day weekend. Check website for schedule. Fee charged.

Mine clubhouse with interpretive exhibits. Open F–Sa, Memorial Day weekend–Labor Day weekend. Free.

3 Hull Rust Mahoning Mine: Hibbing

From Hibbing, continue another 15 miles northeast on Highway 169. Hibbing Chamber of Commerce: 218-262-3895; www.hibbing.org or www.irontrail.org; Hull Rust Mine/Mine View: 218-262-4900 or 218-262-4166 (tourist center)

Called the "Grand Canyon of the North," Hibbing's Hull Rust Mahoning Mine is a National Historic Landmark and the largest open-pit mine in the world. Still active, the 8-mile-long, 800-foot-deep pit consists of more than 50 mines. Unbelievable panoramic view from observation deck located on the north side of town; follow 3rd Avenue East. Walking trail, BMX track, RC flying field and information center. Open daily 9 a.m.–5 p.m., mid-May through Sep. Free, but donations welcomed.

NOTE: Known as the **Hill of Three Waters** or the **Triple Divide**, this point of land is the only one of its kind in the U.S. A raindrop falling to earth at precisely this spot could divide three ways and eventually flow to the Atlantic Ocean, the Gulf of Mexico and Hudson Bay. Although it is not publicly accessible due to mining industry operations, the Triple Divide is 2 miles northwest of town.

OPTION

For a truly eerie sight, tour what's left of **North Hibbing** (follow East 3rd Avenue north from downtown Hibbing about 2 miles). The original town relocated in 1918 to make room for the expanding Hull Rust mine. Log haulers towed houses and steam shovels scooped up graves, leaving behind sidewalks, street lamps and signs. Concrete steps on empty lots lead nowhere. • Andrew Anderson and Carl Wickman saw opportunity in the Hibbing move and capitalized on it. The entrepreneurs shuttled people from the old town to the new

GEOLOGY & CAVE TOURS

in their Hupmobile. By charging 15 cents a ride, their business eventually grew into Greyhound Bus Lines. Five historical buses and the Hupmobile are on display at the **Greyhound Bus Museum**, located at 1201 Greyhound Boulevard. Open daily, mid-May through Sep; 218-263-5814; www.greyhoundbusmuseum.org. Wheelchair accessible. Fee charged.
• Visit the **Hibbing Historical Society Museum** (Memorial Building at 5th Avenue and 23rd Street) for an accurate documentation of the town's relocation. Open T–F; 218-263-8522; www.hibbinghistory.com. Free. • Robert Zimmerman (better known as Bob Dylan) grew up in Hibbing. The **Hibbing Public Library** features an exhibit of the legendary singer/songwriter. Open M–F; 218-362-5959; www.hibbing.mn.us. Free.

4 Minnesota Discovery Center: Chisholm

1005 Discovery Way; Minnesota Discovery Center is west of Chisholm on Highway 169; 218-254-7959 or 800-372-6437; www.mndiscoverycenter.com

Perched atop the Glen iron mine, Minnesota Discovery Center is a giant among interpretive centers. Plan to spend an entire day here as it has something for everyone—mining equipment for climbing on, American Indian camps, trapper's cabins, a children's amusement park and a mine-educational 19-hole mini-golf course. Hop the Mesabi Railway Trolley for a 2.5-mile ride along the Glen mine. The trolley stops at the 1915 Glen Depot for a living-history lesson of what life was like for the residents who lived there at the turn of the twentieth century. Open year-round, call for days and times. Wheelchair accessible. Fee charged.

Located within Minnesota Discovery Center is the **Iron Range Research Library and Archives**. The library contains one of the largest collections of genealogical and local history research materials in the Upper Midwest. Open year-round; 218-254-7959; www.mndiscoverycenter.org.

OPTION

If you're interested in learning how a real mine operates, take the 90-minute **Hibbing Taconite Company Mine Tour**. Tours offered mid-Jun through mid-Aug, Thursdays at 1 p.m. Wear slacks and closed-toe shoes. Must be at least 10 years of age.

Call Minnesota Discovery Center for details; 218-254-7959. Fee charged. • The **Minnesota Museum of Mining** is located in Memorial Park at the top of Main Street. This is a hands-on museum with exhibits indoors and out, as well as a replica of an underground mine and model steam train. Climb aboard a 125-ton dump truck. Also see a 1910 Atlantic steam shovel and a 1907 locomotive. Open Memorial Day–Labor Day, M–Sa, 9–5, Su 1–5; 218-254-5543; www.mnmuseumofmining.org. Fee charged.

5 USS/Minntac: Mountain Iron

Mountain Iron is less than 15 miles east of Chisholm on Highway 169; watch for signs.

Mountain Iron is the birthplace of mining on the Mesabi Iron Range—the 1890 discovery of iron ore there launched the era to come. USS/Minntac is the largest operating taconite plant in Minnesota. From the overlooks, watch 37-cubic-yard shovels load 240-ton trucks. Wacootah and Minntac Mine Overlooks are located at the north end of Mountain Avenue.

6 Leonidas Overlook: Eveleth

Drive south from Virginia for 5 miles on Highway 53
www.ironrange.org/attractions/leonidas-overlook

Leonidas Overlook is the highest man-made point on the Iron Trail and provides a panoramic view of the Cliff's Natural Resources mine.

OPTION

Need a little break from all the mine touring? Then visit the **United States Hockey Hall of Fame Museum** in Eveleth. Inspect jerseys and memorabilia from over 100 hockey greats. Watch recorded scenes from the 1980 "miracle on ice" U.S. Olympic Hockey game. Located along Highway 53 on Hat Trick Avenue; 218-744-5167 or 800-443-7825; www.ushockeyhall.com. Gift shop. Wheelchair accessible. Fee charged.
• Eveleth also boasts the **World's Largest Free-standing Hockey Stick**. It measures 110 feet with a weight over five tons! Downtown district.

7 Iron Trail: Biwabik

From Eveleth, retrace route north on Highway 53 toward Virginia; take Highway 135 northeast; 218-865-4183; www.cityofbiwabik.com

Still part of the Iron Trail, Biwabik is best known for its phenomenal all-season outdoor recreation. With over 2,000 miles of scenic groomed trails and an average snowfall of 100 inches, countless snowmobile magazines proclaim the area a snowmobiler's paradise.

GEOLOGY & CAVE TOURS

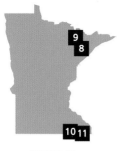

OPTION

Eli Wirtanen Pioneer Farm. Homesteaded in 1904, the self-guided tour consists of 16 buildings including the main house, horse barn, shingle mill and hay shed, along with historical equipment. Fall festival held the second Saturday in September. Half-hour drive south of Biwabik on Highway 4. Watch for signs (farm on the right side of road); 218-638-2859; wirtanenfarm.org. Free.

8 Longyear Drill Site: Hoyt Lakes

Hoyt Lakes; from Biwabik, continue east on Highway 135; turn on Highway 110 (13 miles total); 218-749-3150; www.ironrange.org/attractions/longyear-drill-site

Edmund Longyear introduced diamond drilling to the area in 1890. A quarter-mile wilderness path leads to the Longyear Drill Site. See the actual steam engine used to drive the drill thousands of feet below the surface. Open year-round. No admission fee.

9 Lake Vermilion-Soudan Underground Mine State Park: Soudan

Retrace route to Highway 135. Follow Highway 135 north; go east on Highway 169; 218-300-7000; www.dnr.state.mn.us/state_parks/lake_vermilion_soudan

The Soudan Underground Mine State Park is home to Minnesota's oldest and deepest (27 levels) underground iron mining sites. The 90-minute tour includes an mine-hoist ride that drops a half mile underground, using two spiral staircases and an electric train ride as fun as anything you'll find at Disneyland. A self-guided surface tour includes a drill shop, an engine house, a crusher and a dry house. Visitor center offers informative movie on mining history. Park is off of Highway 169, with plenty of signs pointing the way. Open daily Memorial Day weekend–Labor Day and some days in October; 218-753-2245. Fee charged, free for children under 5.

NOTE: Wear warm clothing. The wind and 50-degree temperature in the mine shaft make for a chilly train ride.

SOUTHEASTERN MINNESOTA'S BLUFF COUNTRY

Explore two caves: Mystery Cave in Forestville State Park, and Niagara Cave in Harmony. From the Twin Cities, take Highway 52 south to Harmony (approximately 140 miles).

10 Mystery Cave

Forestville/Mystery Cave State Park. From Highway 16, follow County 5 south to the cave. Watch for signs; 507-937-3251; www.dnr.state.mn.us/state_parks/forestville_mystery_cave/index.html

Mystery Cave is Minnesota's longest cave. It has 13 miles of natural passages, two levels, clear blue pools, formations and fossils. The 1-hour Scenic Tour has concrete ramps and walkways, and there are many other guided tours to choose from, of varying length and level of challenge. Open Memorial Day–Labor Day, 10 a.m.–5 p.m. Spring and fall, weekends only. Fee charged.

OPTION

Forestville/Mystery Cave State Park has 20 miles of trails through 3,000 acres of wooded ridges and valleys—Minnesota's most popular horse trails. Bring a rod and reel and try your luck in the trout streams. Camping available. • While you're in the park, take a self-guided tour through **Historic Forestville**. Once a thriving rural trade center of 100 residents, Forestville is now a living-history museum. However, a fair word of warning: once you cross the bridge, you're back in 1899. The villagers think cameras are some type of music box! Memorial Day–Labor Day, Th–Su; May, Sep–Oct, Sa only; 507-765-2785; sites.mnhs.org/historic-sites/historic-forestville. State park permit required. Fee charged. • **Spring Valley** is only a few short miles west of Forestville on the junction of Highways 63 & 16. Tour the historic Methodist Church, which was built in the 1870s, where Almanzo and Little House series author Laura Ingalls Wilder attended Sunday services; 221 West Courtland Street; 507-346-7659. Open Jun–Aug; Sep–Oct, weekends only. Fee charged.

11 Niagara Cave

Located 2 miles south of Harmony on Highway 139; then 2 miles west on Niagara Cave Road; 507-886-6606; www.niagaracave.com

The Niagara Cave tour has it all: a roaring waterfall, an underground waterfall and wishing well, a chapel room, stalactites, stalagmites, fossils, pitted limestone walls with about 100-foot-high ceilings, but absolutely no bats. You'll feel as though you're on a hike through the Grand Canyon. Year-round temperature is 48 degrees, so bundle up

and wear comfortable shoes. Gift shop, gemstone mining, picnic facilities and mini-golf course. Guided tours Memorial Day–Labor Day, daily. Fee charged. Ages 3 and under free.

OPTION

About 700 Amish folks live in Harmony's surrounding rural area. Choose from several **tours** offered to learn more about their way of life. Amish Tours of Harmony: 507-886-2303; www.amish-tours.com. Fee charged. R & M Amish Tours: 507-467-2128; www.rmamish.com. Two-hour tour. Fee charged. • Travel the **Amish Buggy Byway** along Highway 52 between Preston and Prosper (just north of the Iowa border). Many Amish farms and horse-drawn buggies along this route; farms dot the landscape.

TWIN CITIES CAVES

12 Battle Creek Park

2300 Upper Afton Road, Maplewood; 651-748-2500;
www.ramseycounty.us/residents/parks-recreation

Take a picnic basket and plenty of energy because you'll want to explore every inch of this park. Lots of good hiking trails and caves, caves, caves!

13 Wabasha Street Caves

215 Wabasha Street South (on the right after the bridge), St. Paul;
651-224-1191; www.wabashastreetcaves.com

St. Paul has a dark past. In the 1930s, notorious gangsters like Ma Barker, Babyface Nelson and John Dillinger terrorized local businesses and citizens. A popular thug hideout was the Wabasha Street Caves. History comes alive with one look at the fireplace marred by bullet holes. Tours year-round, call for hours. Check website for special events. Also offered is a 2-hour tour of **gangster-associated sites**. Fee charged. Cash only.

OPTION

While you're in the area, take a cruise on a paddleboat operated by **Padelford Riverboats**. Daily cruises from Harriet Island on the Mississippi River. Fee charged, free for children age 2 and under. Other trips offered include lunch and dinner cruises, Sunday brunches and fall colors cruises. But that's not all. You can also take in a real theatrical show on a paddleboat. Check website or call for more information on cruises and shows; 800-543-3908 or 651-227-1100; www.riverrides.com.

WESTERN WISCONSIN'S PIERCE COUNTY

Pierce County is home to the largest earthen dam in the Midwest and the longest natural cave in Wisconsin. Pack a picnic basket and pan for gold at Nugget Lake!

14 Crystal Cave

W965 State Road 29, Spring Valley, WI; 800-236-2283; www.acoolcave.com

Open to the public since 1942, Crystal Cave is Wisconsin's longest cave. Tour multiple levels filled with stalactites, stalagmites, dripstone, curtains and helictites. If your prospecting luck at Nugget Lake (pg. 68) was less than successful, buy a bag of gem stock and pan it in the sluice trough. Hour-long guided tours offered daily Apr–Oct. Check website for hours. The gift shop has all kinds of bat paraphernalia, fossils and jewelry, and includes one of the Midwest's largest rock shops. They also have a picnic area and an interpretive trail. Fee charged.

15 Eau Galle Dam

U.S. Army Corps of Engineers, Eau Galle Lake, Spring Valley, WI. From Highway 29, turn onto Van Buren Road. Drive 1 mile to intersection of County B. Cross B and follow park signs; 715-778-5562

In 1943, famous architect Frank Lloyd Wright offered to design a new type of village for Spring Valley, which was prone to repeated flooding. Wright proposed a town under one roof, or "mall" as they're known today. Had the folks taken him up on his offer, it would have been the first in existence by 13 years. Instead, the Army Corps of Engineers came up with a flood control plan, resulting in the construction of the Eau Galle Dam.

At 122 feet tall and 1,800 feet long, Eau Galle Dam is the largest earthen dam of this type in the Midwest. Completed in 1968, the project required more than 2 million cubic yards of rock and fill. The scenic overlook provides a great view of the dam and town below. The tall brick tower near the athletic fields is the remains of an early-twentieth-century iron ore smelter.

Eau Galle Lake offers picnicking, swimming, hiking, fishing (electric motors only), camping and nature programs. Day use fee charged.

16

OPTION

If you're interested in the extraterrestrial, visit Elmwood, WI, the **UFO capital of the world**. Located south of Spring Valley on Highway 128, for some unknown reason this village of 800 folks attracts more than its share of visitors from outer space. Look for commemorative markers along the roadsides.

16 Nugget Lake County Park

N4351 County Road HH, Plum City, WI. Located 31 miles from Prescott. Travel east on Highway 10 through Ellsworth toward Plum City. Watch for signs; 715-639-5611; www.co.pierce.wi.us

From 1887 to 1906, the Land Flour Gold Mining Company operated a placer mine (mechanical way to pan for gold) on Plum Creek, now the north end of the 750-acre Nugget Lake County Park. Open year-round, the picturesque park offers camping, fishing, picnicking, boating (electric motors only), canoeing, kayaking, hiking, nature programs, an outdoor amphitheater, cross-country ski trails and sledding hill.

Licenses, bait, ice, canoe, kayak and boat rentals available at the park office. If you plan to do some prospecting by hand, you can do so if you bring your own pan. Entrance fee per vehicle.

Virginia, Minnesota

Fort Snelling

Man's future is determined by how well he learns from the past.
Nowhere are these lessons catalogued with more passion than in our
museums and art. Many of the historical sites found in this chapter
provide opportunities for you to partake in past events through the
talented efforts of costumed interpreters.

MUSEUMS, HISTORIC SITES & THE ARTS

NORTHERN MUSEUMS

Bonanzaville, *West Fargo, ND.* 72

Children's Museum at Yunker Farm, *Fargo, ND* 72

Comstock House, *Moorhead* 72

Fargo-Moorhead Visitors' Center, *Fargo, ND* 73

Historical & Cultural Society of Clay County, *Moorhead* 73
Option: Bergquist Pioneer Cabin

Roger Maris Museum, *Fargo, ND* 73

Rourke Art Museum, *Moorhead* 74

TWIN CITIES AREA

American Swedish Institute, *Minneapolis* 74

Bell Museum of Natural History, *Minneapolis* 74

Fort Snelling, *St. Paul* 74

Frederick R. Weisman Art Museum, *Minneapolis* 75

James J. Hill House, *St. Paul* 75

Minneapolis Institute of Art, *Minneapolis* 75

Minnesota History Center, *St. Paul* 75
Option: Minnesota State Capitol

Minnesota Museum of American Art, *St. Paul* 76

Oliver H. Kelley Farm, *Elk River* 76

Sibley Historic Site, *Mendota* 76

The Landing (formerly Murphy's), *Shakopee.* 77
Option: Renaissance Festival

Walker Art Center, *Minneapolis* 77

NORTHERN MUSEUMS

Originally settled by Scandinavian immigrants, the Red River Valley is one of the flattest land surfaces in North America, as well as one of the most fertile farming regions in the world. The metro area of Fargo-Moorhead and surrounding communities has a combined population of approximately 228,000 and an impressive number of museums and galleries.

1 Bonanzaville

1351 West Main Avenue, West Fargo, ND; 701-282-2822; www.bonanzaville.org

Tour 15 acres of historical buildings including a sod house, church, courthouse and country store. Also antique cars, airplanes and farm equipment. Costumed interpreters on hand to answer questions. Concessions. Wheelchair accessible. Call for hours. Fee charged.

2 Children's Museum at Yunker Farm

1201 28th Avenue North, Fargo, ND; 701-232-6102; childrensmuseum-yunker.org

The Children's Museum at Yunker Farm features more than 50 hands-on exhibits, including a miniature train and carousel. Self-guided tours. Open daily during summer. Closed Mondays, Labor Day–Memorial weekend. Wheelchair accessible. Fee charged.

3 Comstock House

506 8th Street South, Moorhead, MN; 218-291-4211; sites.mnhs.org/historic-sites/comstock-house

The 1882 Victorian Comstock House was the home of former state senator Solomon G. Comstock. Original furnishings, as well as the family's china, books and clothing. Open Sa–Su during summer and Saturdays from Labor Day–Memorial weekend. Self-guided tours. Wheelchair accessible on first floor. Fee charged.

4 Fargo-Moorhead Visitors' Center

2001 44th Street (the "grain elevator" at exit 348 off of I-94), Fargo, ND; 800-235-7654 or 701-282-3653; www.fargomoorhead.org

Hollywood in Fargo? You betcha! The Red River Valley has its own Celebrity Walk of Fame located in the courtyard of the Visitors' Center. Garth Brooks, KISS, Neil Diamond, Aerosmith, George W. Bush, Dr. Ruth and many more star celebrities have their signatures, footprints and handprints set in cement. Pick up a free state map at the desk. Call for hours.

5 Historical & Cultural Society of Clay County

Hjemkomst Center, 202 1st Avenue North, Moorhead, MN; 218-299-5511; www.hcscconline.org

An award-winning documentary chronicles the construction of this 76-foot-long, hand-built replica of a Viking ship and its 6,000-mile voyage across the Atlantic in 1982. The ship is on display at the Historical & Cultural Society of Clay County; the site also boasts four floors of local history and art exhibits.

Also on display is a replica **Hopperstad Norwegian Stave Church**. Long log columns are the central supports. Guided tours. Wheelchair accessible. Fee charged.

OPTION

Bergquist Pioneer Cabin, 11th Street North, Moorhead, MN; 218-299-5511. Built in 1870, see Moorhead's oldest house still located on its original site. Open third weekend in June.

6 Roger Maris Museum

3902 13th Avenue South, West Acres Shopping Center, intersection of I-29 and 13th Avenue, Fargo, ND; 701-282-2222; www.rogermarismuseum.com

Roger Maris—Fargo native and New York Yankee—hit 61 home runs during the 1961 season, besting Babe Ruth's long-standing record by one. Maris' uniforms, baseball equipment, awards and film footage of his last 12 homers from the 1961 season on exhibit at the West Acres Shopping Center. Concessions. Wheelchair accessible. Call for hours. Free.

7 Rourke Art Museum

521 Main Avenue, Moorhead, MN; 218-236-8861; www.rourkeart.org

The museum (once the Moorhead Post Office) houses permanent collections of contemporary American, pre-Columbian, Hispanic, African and American Indian art. Permanent and changing exhibits. Open F–Su. Guided tours available. Wheelchair accessible. Fee charged.

TWIN CITIES AREA

8 American Swedish Institute

2600 Park Avenue, Minneapolis; 612-871-4907; ASImn.org

This 1908 castle-like structure was the home of Swan J. Turnblad, a Swedish immigrant who made his fortune in the newspaper business. The 33-room castle is now a Swedish American cultural center. Elaborate woodcarvings and plasterwork, antique furnishings, 11 tile stoves and rotating exhibitions. Library, archives, award-winning FIKA café, museum store (items in English and all the Scandinavian languages). Special programs and concerts. Open year-round, call for hours. Fee charged.

9 Bell Museum of Natural History

10 Church Street (University of Minnesota campus), Minneapolis; 612-626-9660; www.bellmuseum.umn.edu/visit/hours-admission

The Bell Museum has hands-on exhibits for children and adults. Lifelike animal and plant displays. Wheelchair accessible. Fee charged.

10 Fort Snelling

Located between the Mississippi River and the Minneapolis-St. Paul International Airport at the junction of Highways 5 & 55, St. Paul; 612-726-1171 www.historicfortsnelling.org

Restored historic Fort Snelling opens its gates and welcomes you to nineteenth-century frontier life. Talk with soldiers who grumble about farm chores. Help with the laundry using a washboard and lye soap. Meet the Dakota wife of a trader or have tea with Mrs. Snelling.

Watch the blacksmith at his forge. Learn how to shoulder a musket, mend clothes. In short, partake in everyday life at the fort. Check website for days and hours. Exhibits, films and gift shop. Cannon shoot. Wheelchair accessible. Fee charged.

11 Frederick R. Weisman Art Museum

333 East River Road (University of Minnesota campus), Minneapolis; 612-625-9494; www.weisman.umn.edu

Find the only odd-shaped, stainless steel-wrapped building in the Twin Cities and you'll have found the Weisman. Known for its bold sculptures, contemporary paintings and imaginative exhibits. Put your ear to a door and do some legal eavesdropping at an exhibit simulating a hotel hallway. Closed Mondays. Gift shop. Wheelchair accessible. Free.

12 James J. Hill House

240 Summit Avenue (½ block west of the Cathedral), St. Paul; 651-297-2555; sites.mnhs.org/historic-sites/james-j-hill-house/james-j-hill

The 1891 James J. Hill House has 4 floors, 42 rooms, 22 fireplaces, 13 bathrooms, a 100-foot reception hall, a skylit art gallery, carved woodwork and stained glass. At the time, this massive stone building was the largest and most expensive private home in the state. A guided tour tells about owner James J. Hill's life and his transportation empire—the Great Northern Railway. Open year-round, reservations recommended. Wheelchair accessible. Fee charged.

13 Minneapolis Institute of Art

2400 3rd Avenue South, Minneapolis; 612-870-3131 or 888-MIA-ARTS; www.artsmia.org

The Minneapolis Institute of Art houses the nation's best Asian art, as well as more than 90,000 other objects. The collection represents artistic traditions and treasures spanning 5,000 years. Closed Mondays. Restaurant, coffee shop, gift shop. Wheelchair accessible. Free except for special exhibits.

14 Minnesota History Center

345 Kellogg Boulevard West, on the corner of Kellogg and John Ireland Boulevards in downtown St. Paul; 888-727-8386 or 651-259-3000; www.minnesotahistorycenter.org

The state's events come alive at the Minnesota History Center. Animated displays, hands-on exhibits—you'll have so much fun, you won't even realize you're in a history center. Open year-round

T–Su and on Monday holidays. Also open Mondays during summer months. Restaurant, gift shop, library, genealogy collection. Wheelchair accessible. Fee charged.

OPTION

The **Minnesota State Capitol** is within walking distance of the Minnesota History Center. See its famous statue with four golden horses, its soaring domes, arches and columns, statues and symbolic murals. For details about tours and a visit: sites.mnhs.org/historic-sites/minnesota-state-capitol. Restaurant, open when in session. Wheelchair accessible.

15 Minnesota Museum of American Art

141 East 4th Street, St. Paul; 651-797-2571; www.mmaa.org

The Minnesota Museum of American Art houses paintings by well-known artists such as Thomas Hart Benton, Childe Hassam and Grant Wood. Open Th–Su. Wheelchair accessible. Free.

16 Oliver H. Kelley Farm

15788 Kelley Farm Road, Elk River; 763- 441-6896; sites.mnhs.org/historic-sites/oliver-h-kelley-farm

Try your hand at 1800s farming at the 189-acre Oliver H. Kelley Farm. Costumed interpreters won't mind if you want to take a turn plowing with oxen or threshing the grain. Partake in the household chores of churning butter, washing laundry with a scrub board and cooking on a wood stove. Nature trails follow the Mississippi River through woods and restored prairies. Open May–Oct. Check website for days and hours. Wheelchair accessible. Fee charged.

17 Sibley Historic Site

1357 Sibley Memorial Highway (Highway 13 northeast of the Mendota bridge and across the river from Fort Snelling), Mendota; 651-452-1596; www.dakotahistory.org

The Sibley Historic Site is Minnesota's oldest European-American settlement. Learn about the life of Henry Sibley, the state's first governor. Explore two 1830s limestone houses, a fur company cold store and the Jean Baptiste Faribault Hotel. Open weekends Memorial Day to Labor Day. Fee charged, free for children ages 5 and under.

18 The Landing (formerly Murphy's)

2187 East Highway 101, Shakopee (located 1 mile east of Shakopee on Highway 101); 763-694-7784
www.threeriversparks.org/parks/the-landing.aspx

A park that preserves Minnesota's early history, the Landing is replete with trails and great views of historic buildings. Visiting the park is free year-round, but in the holiday season, there's a special treat. For a fee, you get a guided tour of inside the houses from a costumed historical interpreter. See website for details and hours.

OPTION

If you happen to be in the area during August and September, check out the **Renaissance Festival**, located 3 miles south of Shakopee on Highway 169. This is sixteenth-century pageantry combined with rowdy fun! Full-contact armored jousting, live mermaids, damsels in distress and nobles of the royal court. Wander the authentic village marketplace where close to 300 artisans hawk their handcrafted goods. Gnaw on a turkey drumstick while enjoying the antics of comedians Puke and Snot. Magicians, jugglers, musicians and more; Aug–Sep, weekends only. Free parking. Wheelchair accessible. Fee charged; 800-966-8215; www.renaissancefest.com.

19 Walker Art Center

1750 Hennepin Avenue, Minneapolis; 612-375-7600; www.walkerart.org

The newly expanded art museum features permanent collections of twentieth-century paintings, sculptures, video art, and photographs, as well as three restaurants, gift shop, library, state-of-the-art theater and cinema. (Check out Gallery 9. The works of more than 100 artists have been featured there since 1997; gallery9.walkerart.org.) Free gallery and architecture tours (with paid gallery admission), Th–Su. Garden tours Sa–Su. The gallery is closed on Monday. Call for a schedule of upcoming live performances and events. Fee charged. Free admission Thursday evenings and the first Saturday of each month. Free for children age 12 and under.

The Walker Art Center is also home to the adjoining 11-acre Minneapolis Sculpture Garden with its Spoonbridge and Cherry. The garden is open daily 6 a.m.–midnight. Free admission.

Mayo Clinic

Rochester is home to 110,000 people, the world-renowned Mayo Clinic, numerous golf courses (do doctors live here or what?), an extensive parks system, the largest IBM complex under one roof, sports, theater, an international airport, top-notch restaurants and shopping. Named one of the three most livable cities in America by *Money Magazine*, Rochester has got it all!

For information, call the Rochester Convention and Visitors Bureau: 800-634-8277 or 507-288-4331; www.rochestercvb.org or www.visitrochestermn.com.

ROCHESTER

TOURING ROCHESTER'S HIGHLIGHTS

Heritage House Victorian Museum 80
Mayo Clinic Hospital. 80
Mayowood Mansion 80
Plummer Building. 80
Plummer House of the Arts 81
Quarry Hill Nature Center 81
Rochester Art Center 81
Silver Lake Park 81
The History Center of Olmsted County 82

Near Rochester: Byron & Mantorville. 82

TOURING ROCHESTER'S HIGHLIGHTS

From the Twin Cities, drive south approximately 80 miles on Highway 52.

1 Heritage House Victorian Museum

255 1st Avenue Northwest; 507-286-9208; www.heritagehousevictorianmuseum.com

Heritage House Victorian Museum offers a glimpse of what life was like for a middle-class Midwestern family over a century ago. Check website for days and hours. Fee charged.

2 Mayo Clinic Hospital

Saint Marys Campus: 1216 2nd Street Southwest; www.mayoclinic.org/saintmaryshospital

Methodist Campus: 201 West Center Street; www.mayoclinic.org/methodisthospital

Self-guided tours, tour brochures available at information desks.

3 Mayowood Mansion

3720 Mayowood Road Southwest; 507-282-9447; www.olmstedhistory.com/mayowood-mansion

The gorgeous, 48-room Mayowood Mansion was home to three generations of Mayos. Furniture, antiques and Mayo family mementos. Expansive grounds, beautiful gardens. Tours from mid-Apr to Oct. Check website for days and hours. Fee charged.

4 Plummer Building

2nd Avenue and 2nd Street Southwest (across from the Mayo Building); 507-284-8294

Housed in the tower of the Plummer Building, the 56-bell Rochester Carillon covers a $4\frac{1}{2}$ octave range. The largest bell weighs over 7,800 pounds. Third-floor tours of the original offices of founding Drs. William J. and Charles H. Mayo are offered to patients and guests only, but tours of the carillon are available if you call and schedule ahead. Open M–F. Free.

5 Plummer House of the Arts

1091 Plummer Lane Southwest; 507-328-2525; www.rochestermn.gov/depart
ments/parks-and-recreation/indoor-facilities/plummer-house

The 49-room Tudor mansion was the home of Dr. Henry S. Plummer,
the innovator credited for the Mayo's lift systems, pneumatic tubes
and accessible medical records. Plummer installed many state-of-
the-art gadgets of the time in his home, such as a central vacuum,
garage door openers, a gas furnace and an intercom system. Eleven
landscaped acres, formal gardens, bird trail, quarry and water tower.
Grounds open year-round. Tours Jun–Aug, Wednesdays. Fee charged.

6 Quarry Hill Nature Center

Quarry Hill Nature Center, 701 Silver Creek Road Northeast. Located on
the northeast edge of Rochester. Take County 22 to Silver Creek Road;
507-281-6114; www.qhnc.org

Quarry Hill Nature Center is located in 329-acre Quarry Hill Park
and offers more than 8 miles of paved and grassy trails, a 3-acre
pond, historic sandstone cave and fossil quarry. The nature center
features interactive displays, live animals and exhibits, including a
1,700-gallon native fish aquarium, indoor honeybee observation hive
and a life-sized model of a *T. rex* skull. Summer nature day-camp and
year-round naturalist programs. Seasonal ski and snowshoe rental.
Open daily, year-round. Free admission.

7 Rochester Art Center

40 Civic Center Drive Southeast; 507-282-8629; www.rochesterartcenter.org

The Rochester Art Center features fine arts and crafts as well as
changing exhibits. On Thursday evenings the Art Center sponsors a
series of videos showcasing artists and their work. Open year-round.
Free, but donation suggested.

8 Silver Lake Park

North Broadway; 800-634-8277 or 507-288-4331 (Rochester Convention and
Visitors Bureau); silverlakefun.com

Outdoor pool, skate park, playground equipment, picnic facilities.
Bike, paddleboat, canoe and kayak rental. Open year-round.

9-10

9 ▎ The History Center of Olmsted County

1195 West Circle Drive Southwest; 507-282-9447; www.olmstedhistory.com

Learn the story behind Rochester's rise as a global leader in health care through exhibits at the The History Center of Olmsted County. Open year-round. Closed Su–M and all major holidays.

Explore the 1862 William Dee Log Cabin, Hadley Valley School House and the George Stoppel Farm (est. 1856). Open Memorial Day–Labor Day. Free (donation suggested).

10 ▎ Near Rochester: Byron & Mantorville

Byron: Oxbow Park and **Zollman Zoo** (15-minute drive from Rochester)—take Highway 14 west to Byron, turn north on County 5, go 3 miles, watch for signs. Oxbow Park and Zollman Zoo offer wooded hiking and cross-country ski trails, a picturesque stream with bridges, playground equipment, picnic facilities and nature center; 507-775-2451; www.co.olmsted.mn.us/pw/parks/oxbowpark. Zoo is free, but donations are welcomed.

Mantorville: Mantorville is 17 miles from Rochester. Take Highway 14 west to Kasson, then go 3 miles north on Highway 57; www.mantorville.com. A town of 1,200, **Historic Mantorville** features a covered bridge, antiques and gift shops, fine dining and plenty of nostalgic charm.

Once a stagecoach stop, the 1856 **Hubbell House** restaurant has served such celebrities as Mickey Mantle, Dwight Eisenhower and Roy Rogers. Wonderful food, Civil War-era decor. On the main drag in Mantorville; 507-635-2331; www.hubbellhouserestaurant.com. Closed Mondays.

Let your nose lead you to **The Chocolate Shoppe**. They also sell fresh fudge and truffles, and numerous flavors of jelly beans, taffy and other candies. Try their chocolate-covered potato chips. They also sell 40 different flavors of jelly beans, taffy and other candies. On Main Street, on the corner across from the Hubbell House. Closed Mondays; 507-635-5814.

Once a grocery store, **Memorabilia** now stocks the meat and produce coolers with antique spice cans and glassware. Nice displays featuring full china sets and antique stemware. You'll feel as if you've been invited to a formal dinner party. Furniture and more. Memorabilia is next to the Opera House; 507-635-5419.

Make a night of it and see a live performance by the **Mantorville Theatre Company** in the Historic Opera House. Box office opens one hour before showtime. Open year-round. See website for schedule; 507-635-5420; www.mantorvillain.com. Fee charged.

Hot air ballooning over the St. Croix River

The whole world loves a lover, and that must go double for a couple in love! To keep the fires of passion burning, stoke them often with the romantic getaways found in this chapter. Each enchanting trip is filled with picturesque small towns, lazy strolls, candlelit evenings and plenty of opportunity to romance the one you love.

ROMANTIC GETAWAYS

EXCELSIOR
Excelsior Streetcar Line 86

Steamboat Minnehaha 86

The Old Log Theater. 86

STILLWATER
Aamodt's Hot Air Balloon Ride. 87
Options: Freight House Restaurant, Stillwater Trolley, Gondola Romantica

Aurora Staples Inn 87

Lowell Inn. 88

The Englishman's Carriage House B&B 88

TAYLORS FALLS
Folsom House. 88
Option: Angel Hill Historic District

Franconia Sculpture Park 89
Option: Osceola & St. Croix Valley Railway

Interstate State Park. 89

Old Jail Bed & Breakfast. 89

PRESCOTT, WISCONSIN
Muddy Waters 90
Option: Vino in the Valley

Welcome & Heritage Center 90

EXCELSIOR

Excelsior is located about 20 minutes west of the Twin Cities on Highway 7. Visit Excelsior's website at www.excelsior-lakeminnetonkachamber.com.

1 Excelsior Streetcar Line

Water Street; 952-922-1096; www.trolleyride.org

If boats aren't for you, then take a 1-mile ride on Car No. 78—one of the oldest operating, museum-quality trolleys in the country. The 10-minute ride aboard the beautifully restored yellow streetcar is a journey back to the turn of the twentieth century. Catch the streetcar at Water Street. Check website for schedule. Fee charged.

2 Steamboat Minnehaha

Water Street; 952-474-2115; www.steamboatminnehaha.org

Enjoy the scenery aboard the restored 1905 steamboat Minnehaha as she travels across Lake Minnetonka to Wayzata. Get off and look around or return to Excelsior. Visit website for days and hours. Board at the dock on Water Street. Purchase tickets online or on the boat.

3 The Old Log Theater

5185 Meadville Street; 952-474-5951 or 866-653-5641; www.oldlog.com

As the sun slips below the horizon, the lakeside trees come alive with sparkling white lights. End the day with a romantic dinner for two and a live performance at The Old Log Theater—one of the oldest continuously running theaters in the country. Wheelchair accessible. Call for reservations.

STILLWATER

Directions: A short 20-minute drive from the Twin Cities. Take I-94 east to Highway 95 north. Another option is Highway 36 east. Greater Stillwater Chamber of Commerce: 651-439-4001; greaterstillwaterchamber.com

4 Aamodt's Hot Air Balloon Rides

6428 Manning Avenue North; 651-351-0101; www.aamodtsballoons.com

What could be more romantic than floating away together in one of Aamodt's hot air balloons? Experience this peaceful way to travel the scenic river valley while your pilot points out interesting sights. The 60-minute ride departs 3 miles west of Stillwater at Aamodt's Apple Farm, then return for a champagne toast. Fee charged.

OPTION

Once back in Stillwater, take a leisurely stroll along the river-front. Watch the lift bridge in action, enjoy the gardens and shop the boutiques. Spend a pleasant hour or two dining on the open deck at the **Freight House Restaurant**, found along the river's edge; 651-439-5718; www.thefreighthouse. com • Board the **Stillwater Trolley** for a 45-minute narrated tour, and learn about what was once the largest lumber community in the country. A drive by Stillwater's beautifully restored homes is included on the trolley route. Open May–Oct, daily. Board near the Freight House; 651-430-0352; www.stillwatertrolley.com. See website for schedule. Fee charged. • **Gondola Romantica**, Stillwater public dock; 651-439-1783; www.gondolaromantica.com. Nothing spells romance like an Italian serenade while gliding down the St. Croix nestled in a gondola from Venice. Gondola Romantica offers a glimpse into the Venetian world as it was a millennium ago. Bring a picnic lunch or have them arrange something special for you. Rides range from 45 minutes to 1 hour and seat up to six. Open May–Oct, weather permitting. Call or visit website to schedule a cruise. Fee charged.

5 Aurora Staples Inn

303 North 4th Street; 651-351-1187; www.aurorastaplesinn.com

Stillwater is an antiquer's paradise. With so many interesting shops to poke around in, it's a real challenge to visit them all. Thank heavens you reserved a room at the Aurora Staples Inn and don't have to try to fit everything into one day. This 1892 Victorian mansion overlooks the St. Croix River. A wraparound porch, formal gardens, an open oak staircase and five rooms with private baths, whirlpools and fireplaces. Full breakfast. Also open for tours.

6 Lowell Inn

102 North 2nd Street, Stillwater; 651-439-1100; www.lowellinn.com

After you've had a chance to freshen up a bit, it's time to think about those dinner plans. *Gourmet Magazine* voted the Lowell Inn the most romantic dining experience in the Twin Cities. The Lowell Inn offers three distinct and beautiful dining settings, from very formal (the George Washington Room) to alfresco. The Matterhorn Room serves Swiss Fondue and fantastic wines. Rooms available.

NOTE: Stillwater offers many bed and breakfast accommodations as well as motels. Call the Greater Stillwater Chamber of Commerce for more information; 651-439-4001; greaterstillwaterchamber.com.

7 The Englishman's Carriage House B&B

807 Harriet Street South; 651-430-8008; www.jamesmulveyinn.com

The carriage house was originally built to house the Mulvey's collection of carriages and fine horses; in the later years, it was renovated to become a living quarters for the owner's married children. Today the carriage house resembles an English cottage and provides a uniquely private bed and breakfast experience. In the morning, you'll enjoy breakfast on white linen at the historic Lowell Inn.

TAYLORS FALLS

Taylors Falls is less than an hour's drive from the Twin Cities. Take I-94 east to Highway 95 north. Falls Chamber of Commerce; 715-483-3580; fallschamber.org.

8 Folsom House

272 Government Street, Angel Hill Historic District, Taylors Falls; 651-465-3125; fallschamber.org/history/tf-history

Take a guided tour of lumber baron W. H. C. Folsom's home. The 1855 Greek Revival house has colorful rooms, wood floors and a cheery New England feel. Open from Memorial Day weekend into October. See website for days and hours. Fee charged.

After your tour, do a little sightseeing on your own. Walk or drive past the many other restored homes in the **Angel Hill Historic District**.

9 Franconia Sculpture Park

29836 St. Croix Trail, Franconia (on Highway 8); 651-257-6668; www.franconia.org

Experienced artists from all over the world (and those still wet behind the ears) bring their own unique vision to life at the 43-acre Franconia Sculpture Park. Meet the sculptors, see hundreds of works, and even see cast-metal sculpture demonstrations. Open daily from dawn to dusk.

OPTION

In nearby Osceola, Wisconsin, hop a vintage diesel or steam-powered train for a ride through the rolling hills of the Dairy State, or choose a longer excursion to Marine on St. Croix, MN. Get off and stretch the legs in this captivating river town. Call the scenic **Osceola & St. Croix Valley Railway**, 715-755-3570, or visit www.trainride.org for schedule and fares.

10 Interstate State Park

Taylors Falls on Highway 8 along the St. Croix River; 651-465-5711; www.dnr.state.mn.us/state_parks/interstate/index.html

Pack a lunch and hike the 4 miles of trails in Minnesota's second-oldest state park. Take your time exploring the numerous glacial potholes—one is 60 feet deep and considered the deepest pothole in the world! If you're a rock climber, you'll be in good company as many come to scale Interstate's challenging cliffs. State Park permit required.

Tired of walking? Then take a riverboat excursion, rent a canoe or just park yourself on a nearby 1.1 billion-year-old boulder and soak up the pulsing green landscape. No park permit required for visits only to riverboat company—it is adjacent to park.

11 Old Jail Bed & Breakfast

349 Government Street, Taylors Falls; 651-465-3112; www.oldjail.com

Spend a weekend with the "old ball and chain" in the historic 1884 Jail Cottage, but don't worry—the hearty breakfasts are a delicious far cry from bread and water. You're expected, however, to put up with such things as spaciousness, privacy and beautiful views. If that sounds like your kind of torture, reserve a cell for yourself and a mate.

12-13

PRESCOTT, WISCONSIN

Prescott is approximately 30 miles from the Twin Cities. Take Highway 61 south, then turn east on Highway 10. Prescott Area Chamber of Commerce: 715-262-3284 or www.prescottwi.com.

Prescott is Wisconsin's oldest river town and one of its most romantic. Stroll the charming downtown shops and cafes on Broad Street.

12 Muddy Waters

231 North Broad Street; 715-262-5999; www.muddywatersbarandgrill.biz

This place is loaded with atmosphere and great food. During summer weekends enjoy live blues music in the bar, or eat outdoors on one of their three decks and watch the river traffic float by. Fresh seafood, ribs—smoked on-site, pizzas, pastas and more. Open year-round.

OPTION

Not far from Prescott you'll find **Vino in the Valley**, an open-air pavilion situated in the gorgeous Rush River Valley. The restaurant serves Italian cuisine, brick oven pizzas, and an assortment of wine and beer. Live music, carriage rides, gift shop, bonfires, walking trails along the river; W3826 450th Avenue, Maiden Rock, WI. May–Oct. Check website or call for days and hours; 715-639-6677; www.vinointhevalley.com.

13 Welcome & Heritage Center

Corner of Broad Street and Highway 10 (next to the bridge); 715-262-3284; www.prescottwi.com

Stop in at the Welcome & Heritage Center for free maps and information on the Great River Road and the charming Wisconsin Rustic Road. For those interested in history, the center is a great place to begin Prescott's Historic Walking Tour of 14 sites, including Mercord Mill Park (at the confluence of the St. Croix and Mississippi Rivers) and the 1923 Vertical-Lift Bridge Gearhouse.

St. Croix River, Taylors Falls

It's been said the best antiques are old friends, but that doesn't mean you can't fall in love with a primitive pine bench or a piece of colorful majolica. This chapter shares some of Minnesota's best spots for antiquing in small towns that are as charming and vintage as the wares they sell.

SMALL TOWN ANTIQUING

ANTIQUING THE GREAT RIVER ROAD

Red Wing 96
Options: Red Wing Shoe Store, Hay Creek Stables, Red Wing Stoneware
Company, Cannon Valley Trail, St. James Hotel

Bay City, Wisconsin 97
Options: Flat Pennies Ice Cream, Rush River Produce

Maiden Rock, Wisconsin 97
Option: Smiling Pelican Bakeshop

Stockholm, Wisconsin 98
Option: Stockholm Gardens

Pepin, Wisconsin 98
Options: Sailboat ride, J&J Barbecue

Alma, Wisconsin 99
Options: Rieck's Lake Park, Buena Vista Park, Fire & Ice, Danzinger Vineyards,
Great River Houseboats, Historic Corner Store

Wabasha 100
Options: National Eagle Center, Villa Maria Center, Old Frontenac Historic District

ANTIQUING THE NORTH COUNTRY

Park Rapids 101
Options: Summerhill Farm, Sun Porch, Nevis

Akeley 101

Walker 102

NE BLUFF COUNTRY ANTIQUING

Winona 102
Options: Lake Park, Pickwick Mill

La Crescent 103
Options: Houston, Houston Nature Center, International Owl Center

Lanesboro 104
Option: Commonweal Theatre Company

Preston 104
Options: JailHouse Historic Inn, Historic Forestville, Fountain

Chatfield 105

Rochester 105

Highway 52 Route North—Oronoco 105

Pine Island 106

Cannon Falls. 106
Option: Cannon River Winery

Highway 14 Route West—Eyota 107

St. Charles 107

SW BLUFF COUNTRY ANTIQUING

Spring Grove. 107

Mabel 107

Harmony 108

Austin. 108
Options: Spam Museum, Jay C. Hormel Nature Center, Mower County
Historical Society, The Old Mill Restaurant

Mantorville 109

1-3

ANTIQUING THE GREAT RIVER ROAD

Voted one of the ten most scenic drives in America, traveling the Great River Road (Highway 35) offers more than unparalleled beauty—it's also a great place to hunt antiques. This 100-mile trip crisscrosses Minnesota and Wisconsin. And although it doesn't cover every single antiques shop, it does treat you to many goodies not always on the beaten path; www.wigreatriverroad.org or www.mississippi-river.org.

1 Red Wing

Highway 61 south from the Twin Cities, approximately 50 miles; www.redwing.org

This pretty river town is home to Red Wing Shoes and the birthplace of Red Wing Pottery. For more information, visit the Red Wing Visitors and Convention Bureau (651-385-5934; www.redwing.org), located behind the St. James Hotel in the historic depot.

Pottery Place Antiques, 2000 Old West Main Street; 651-388-7765; www.potteryplaceantiques.com. Open daily. Pottery and vintage glass and books.

Al's Antique Mall, 512 Plum Street. Open daily; 651-388-0572 or 888-388-0572. Features just about everything; 8,000 square feet.

OPTION

See the world's largest boot at the **Red Wing Shoe Store**, 315 Main Street; 651-388-6233. Three levels house 30,000 pairs of shoes and boots, and an interesting museum that documents the famous Red Wing Shoe history. Since we're talking rides, here's another option: **Hay Creek Stables** offer guided trail rides, wagon rides and more; 29491 Hay Creek Trail; 651-385-9395; www.haycreekstables.com • Although the original Red Wing pottery business closed in 1969, the **Red Wing Stoneware Company** bought the reproduction rights and still uses some of the original molds. Open daily, watch potters at work through a window in the showroom. Located on Highway 61 in the industrial park at the west end of town; 800-352-4877 or 651-388-4610; www.redwingstoneware.com

• The **Cannon Valley Trail** connects Red Wing, Welch and Cannon Falls. www.cannonvalleytrail.com. Twenty miles of hiking, biking, in-line skating and cross-country skiing. Pass required, visit website to purchase. No pets. Located 1 block off Highway 61 on Old West Main Street and Bench Street. Parking lot with facilities. • Restored to its Victorian splendor, the nineteenth-century **St. James Hotel** offers pampered overnight stays, fine dining, lunches on the veranda, an English pub and courtyard shopping; 406 Main Street; 800-252-1875 or 651-388-2846; www.st-james-hotel.com.

2 Bay City, Wisconsin

Highway 63. Turn east on Highway 35 and follow to Bay City. Watch for Bald Eagles along the way!

Oldstuff, Highway 35 (renovated gas station at the east end of town). Nice folks with a lot of knowledge of the business and local area. Open year-round by chance. If the sign's out, they're open. Glassware, primitives, collectibles, yard finds.

OPTION

Hop aboard Soo Line Caboose #27 at **Flat Pennies Ice Cream**, W6442 Highway 35; 715-594-3555; www.flatpennies.com. This is a fun stop for a quick sandwich and soft-serve ice cream, or perhaps a doggie treat if you happen to be traveling with a furry friend. Open Mar–Nov. • For the sweetest blueberries and a valley view that won't quit, stop in at **Rush River Produce**. Pick your own, or buy already picked. Look for the sign on Highway 35, turn north onto County A and follow signs. Also gooseberries, currants, tart pie cherries, honey, jams and maple syrup. Seasonal, call or check website for hours and availability; 715-594-3648; rushriverproduce.com.

3 Maiden Rock, Wisconsin

Maiden Rock is 15 miles southeast of Red Wing, MN, on Highway 35.

Maiden Rock's name originates from the legend of a beautiful Dakota girl who chose to leap to her death rather than marry a man she didn't love. The famed rock is less than 5 miles south of town. A historical marker gives the details.

Basil's, Highway 35 (located in the charming mid-nineteenth-century church). Open Su, May–Dec. Call for hours; 651-207-9023. Antiques and gift shop.

OPTION

Look for the **Smiling Pelican Bakeshop** on Highway 35 in a cozy 1870s two-story house. Owner Sandra Theilman's culinary works of art are melt-in-your-mouth delicious. Pies,

4-6

tarts, quiches, scones, muffins, cookies, breads and more. Open Apr–Christmas, F–Su; 715-448-3807.

4 Stockholm, Wisconsin

Stockholm is 21 miles southeast of Red Wing, MN, on Highway 35 (90-minute drive from the Twin Cities); www.stockholmwisconsin.com

You'll lose your heart to this Swedish "Eden"—the tiny town (only 66 folks) with the great gardens and a plethora of distinctive shops all housed within vintage buildings. In fact, the website Travel Wisconsin rated Stockholm as one of the top five shopping destinations in the state. What can you expect to find in Stockholm? Restaurants, bakeries, a winery/cidery, galleries, hand-thrown pottery, gourmet cookware and foods, Amish furniture and gifts, boutiques, Scandinavian gift shop and so much more.

OPTION

Stockholm Gardens, Highway 35 (east end of town); 715-442-3200. Gorgeous display gardens specializing in wildflowers and the unusual. Their hibiscus have dinner plate-sized blooms. Look for the white picket fence. Open daily, mid-Apr to Oct. Call or check website for days and hours; www.stockholmgardens.com.

5 Pepin, Wisconsin

Pepin is 28 miles southeast of Red Wing, MN, on Highway 35.

Pepin is the birthplace of famous children's author Laura Ingalls Wilder. Visitors from around the world sign the guest book noting their pleasure at picnicking on the actual site of Laura's early childhood days.

OPTION

There's plenty to do in this picturesque little town. Head to the marina to sign up for a 2-hour **sailboat ride**; 715-442-2250; www.sailpepin.com. Or browse the many unique shops and galleries. You won't leave the town hungry. Pepin restaurants offer everything from fine dining to bar fare. • The next town south of Pepin is Nelson, WI, where you'll find **J&J Barbecue**. They do it all—catering, ribs, cheese, ribs, ice cream, ribs, antiques, ribs, collectibles, ribs . . . you get the idea; 208 North Main, Nelson; 715-673-4717; www.jandjbbq.com.

SMALL TOWN
ANTIQUING

Alma, Wisconsin

Alma is 44 miles southeast of Red Wing, MN, on Highway 35 (2-hour drive from the Twin Cities); www.almawisconsin.com

Historic Alma is only 2 blocks wide, but 7 miles long. Houses seem as if they're carved from the river bluffs.

Lone Pine Antiques, S1401 Spring Creek Road; 608-685-4839. Turn off of Highway 35 north of Alma (by the school) onto Spring Creek Road; follow for 2 miles winding your way through a picturesque Wisconsin valley. The drive alone is worth taking. A barn and five sheds crammed with glassware, primitives, furniture and yard finds. Open year-round by chance or appointment.

OPTION

Rieck's Lake Park is the perfect spot for some serious eagle watching. Nesting season mid-Mar to mid-Jul. Free year-round viewing scope and eagle information. Park facilities and campground. Rieck's Lake Park is north of Alma on Highway 35; 612-685-3303 • **Buena Vista Park** is 500 feet straight above the Mississippi River. Panoramic view of Alma and the river valley. Awesome sight for those who love heights. Follow sign from Highway 35. Park facilities. Free. • **Fire & Ice**, 305 North Main Street, Alma; 612-423-3653; www.hoteldevillealma.com. The 1868 building is loaded with charm and good things to eat—hand-dipped ice cream cones, gourmet coffees and desserts. Order a bowl of sinfully delicious blueberry cheesecake ice cream and head out back to an amazing "secret garden." The gorgeous Italianate formal garden, carved into the hillside, features fountains, bronze statues and a lovely break from the fast track. Open daily in summer, and weekends May and Sep–Oct. • **Danzinger Vineyards** sits atop the river bluffs and offers spectacular views of the Mississippi River far, far below. Owned and operated by two retired dairy farmers, the 18-acre vineyard has a nice wine selection, tasting room, and an outdoor patio you need to take advantage of; S2015 Grapeview Lane (off of County Road E), Alma; 608-685-6000; www.danzingervineyard.com • **Great River Houseboats**, 125 Beach Harbor Road; 800-982-8410; www.greatriver-houseboats.com. Looking for something really different in lodging? Look no further than the Alma Marina. The houseboats include kitchen, bathroom with shower and can sleep up to ten people. • And since you're already in Fountain City you might as well visit the **Historic Corner Store** at Main and Liberty streets. The store is a combination of old-fashioned soda fountain, coffee shop, odd gifts, and laundromat; 608-687-3313.

7 Wabasha

29 miles south of Red Wing, MN, on Highway 61; 651-565-4158 or www.wabashamn.org or. From Alma, drive north on Highway 35 to Nelson— bridge crosses the Mississippi River into Wabasha.

More than a town of *Grumpy Old Men*, Wabasha has one of the largest wintering concentrations of Bald Eagles in the lower 48 states. Established in the 1830s, Wabasha is Minnesota's oldest town.

Wabasha Discount Market, 201 Industrial Court. Watch for signs. Year-round indoor retail, and outdoor sales, weather permitting; 651-565-4767.

Proud's Bridgeside Antiques, 234 Main Street West; 651-560-4925. Antiques, dishware, clothing, gifts.

On the River Boutique, 257 Main Street West (in Old City Hall); 651-565-3769. Antiques and gifts.

OPTION

National Eagle Center, 50 Pembroke Avenue; 651-565-4989; www.nationaleaglecenter.org. This must-see magnificent complex is home to several resident eagles, hands-on activities, observation decks with spotting scopes, informative guides, gift shop and tons more. Open daily, year-round, fee charged. • **Villa Maria Center**, 29847 County 2 Boulevard, Frontenac; 651-345-4582; www.villamariaretreats.org. Originally a convent school for girls, the Villa Maria is now a conference/retreat center. A "prayer trail" leads through the surrounding woods. Visitors welcome daily. Call for hours. • **Old Frontenac Historic District**. Continue on the road past the Villa Maria Center into Old Frontenac, a mid-nineteenth-century look at Minnesota's past. One-lane gravel paths overlook Lake Pepin with block after block of restored Civil War-era two-story homes, white painted clapboards, green shutters and expansive lawns.

NOTE: If you happen to be in the area during the first weekend in May, you're in for tons of deals, steals and squeals as the entire loop turns into one giant **100-Mile Garage Sale**. Annual event, from dawn to dusk; www.100milegaragesale.org.

ANTIQUING THE NORTH COUNTRY

For antiques lovers, it's as much about the hunt as it is the purchase. A day spent in these small-town gems is surely one you'll treasure.

8 | Park Rapids

Park Rapids' old-fashioned confectioneries, soda fountains, charming shops and vintage Main Street are enough to make any antiques lover swoon. For more information about the city and surrounding communities, contact the Park Rapids Chamber of Commerce at 800-247-0054 or 218-732-4111 or visit www.parkrapids.com.

Linda's Recycled Goods, 807 West 1st Street; 218-732-3949. Open daily, year-round.

Six-Toed Cat Antiques, 808 East 1st Street; 218-732-8919. Open May–Sep, W–Sa. Specializes in American and European art and furniture; www.sixtoedcatantiques.com.

Summerset Outdoor Flea Market, 17770 Highway 34; 218-237-3000. Open Memorial Day–Labor Day, Thursdays, weather permitting.

Toys for Boys, 409 West 1st Street; 218-732-5668. Specialties include '40s- and '50s-era collectibles. James Dean, Marilyn Monroe, Betty Boop and more.

OPTION

Summerhill Farm, 24013 Highway 71 North, Park Rapids; 218-732-3865; www.summerhill-farm.com. Seven unique gift shops featured inside a barn, stable, carriage house, tree house and more. There's also the **Sun Porch** for lunch and delicious desserts. Open daily, mid-May to mid-Sep. • The town of **Nevis** is midpoint on the 49-mile-long Heartland Trail, Minnesota's first rail-to-trail system. The paved trail winds through woods, offering excellent birding and gorgeous lake views. Nevis also boasts the world's largest tiger muskie . . . statue, that is.

9 | Akeley

Abigail's Attic Antiques & Collectibles, 28 East Broadway, Akeley; 612-720-8833; www.abigailsatticantiques.com

Ardele McAlpine, owner of Abigail's Attic Antiques, grew up with "old things." She says, "There's a feeling of warmth and comfort in antiques; they remind me of home." She also loves meeting new people and has a lot of opportunity for it. Her 1,000-square-foot, 1920s white and red-trimmed shop has attracted visitors from every

state in the nation, as well as many foreign countries. It's packed from floor to ceiling with pottery, furniture, vintage toys, dolls, and much more. Open May to mid-Nov. Call or check website for days and hours.

10 Walker

Located on the southwest side of Leech Lake (one of Minnesota's largest lakes), Walker offers scenic beauty, magnificent hiking, biking, horseback trails and great shopping. Bargain hunt at their fantastic "crazy day" sales (held monthly, summer only); www.leech-lake.com.

Heritage Antiques, Village Square Building, 5th & Minnesota; 218-547-3501. Furniture, accessories.

NE BLUFF COUNTRY ANTIQUING

Antiquing the bluff country is unlike any other experience: quaint small towns, rolling wooded hills and valleys. Any time of year is the perfect time to antique and sightsee.

11 Winona

120 miles south of the Twin Cities on Highway 61. Winona Chamber of Commerce, 902 East 2nd Street, Suite 120; 800-657-4972 or 507-452-0735; www.visitwinona.com

Built on a sandbar created by the Mississippi River, Winona calls herself the "Island City." From the vantage of the **Garvin Heights** overlook, it's easy to see why. Travel the 2 miles straight up and have a look for yourself. To get to Garvin Heights, turn south off of Highway 61 on Huff Street (opposite direction of Winona) and follow Garvin Heights Road to overlook.

A-Z Collectibles, 152 Main Street; 507-454-0366. Open M–F and most Sunday afternoons.

Treasures Under Sugar Loaf, 1023 Sugar Loaf Road; 507-474-7030; visitwinona.com/directory-entry/treasures-under-sugar-loaf. Explore the nooks and crannies of the historic Bub's Brewery building and peruse their collection of antiques, collectibles, home décor, jewelry, artifacts and primitives, and creations by local artisans. Tours of the caves that were once used to store beer are scheduled throughout the year. Open year-round. Call or check website for day and hours.

OPTION

Don't miss the gorgeous rose gardens in **Lake Park** located along the riverfront. Band shell, Veterans Memorial, a paved bike and walking trail, paddleboating and canoeing. Take Huff Street to Lake Park Drive • **Pickwick Mill**, take Highway 61 south to County 7 (between Winona and La Crescent); 507-457-0499 or 507-452-9658; www.pickwickmill.org. Charming six-story 1858 limestone mill, waterfall and mill-pond. Open May–Oct, T–Su. Museum and 18-minute film. Fee charged.

12 La Crescent

From Winona, continue south on Highway 61 where the road joins with I-90. Continue south another 7 miles, watch for signs.

Called the "Apple Capital of Minnesota," La Crescent has the Mississippi River on one side, and apple orchard-covered bluffs on the other.

Apple Valley Gifts & Antiques, 329 Main Street; 507-895-4268. Home décor, fashion, kitchen and garden items, antiques and more. Open daily.

OPTION

Houston is approximately 15 miles southwest of La Crescent on Highway 16. It's easy to understand why they call this region "Bluff Country" with its breathtaking scenery, rolling hills and bluffs, hardwood forests and winding roads. Southeastern Minnesota is the only portion of the state that wasn't leveled by glaciers during the Ice Age. Visit the **Houston Nature Center,** 215 West Plum Street—the town's trailhead for the Root River Trail; 507-896-4668; www.houstonnaturecenter.com. Highlights include a 1-acre green and growing natural playground, a woolly mammoth tooth, and a mount of a pair of White-tailed Deer with their antlers locked in mortal combat. Hands-on nature displays, free showers, vehicle shuttle service. A couple blocks from the nature center is the **International Owl Center,** the only owl education center in the country; 126 East Cedar Street; 507-896-6957; www.internationalowlcenter.org. Stop and see the live owls, hands-on displays and special programs. Open year-round, F–M.

13-17

13 Lanesboro

Lanesboro is southwest of Houston on Highway 16. Lanesboro Area Chamber of Commerce, 100 Milwaukee Road; 507-467-2696; www.lanesboro.com

Lanesboro is a treasure trove of history. Nearly the entire downtown district is on the National Register of Historic Places. Flower-lined streets loaded with unique gift shops and restaurants, an old-fashioned ice cream parlor, Root River State Trail, B&Bs and antiques. The first of Buffalo Bill's Wild West Shows was performed in Lanesboro.

Little River General Store, 105 Coffee Street, downtown; 507-467-2943 or 800-994-2943. Open daily, May–Nov. Bicycle sales, repair and rental, and canoe, kayak and tube rentals and shuttle service. Supplies and more; www.lrgeneralstore.net.

OPTION

Commonweal Theatre Company, 208 Parkway North; 800-657-7025 or 507-467-2525; www.commonwealtheatre. org. Experience live, professional theater. Check website for performance schedule.

14 Preston

Preston is southwest of Lanesboro on Highway 16.

Preston is the Fillmore County seat.

OPTION

A stay at Preston's jail would be quite a treat, as long as it's the 1869 **JailHouse Historic Inn**, 109 Houston Street Northwest; 507-765-2181; www.jailhouseinn.com. Twelve rooms with private baths, fireplaces, whirlpools, a two-story porch, full breakfast. The Cell Block suite retains some of its "original" decor. • **Historic Forestville** is roughly 7 miles west of Preston off of Highway 12. Tour the 1890s town complete with costumed interpreters. State Park permit required. NOTE: See the Mystery Cave tour on pg. 65 for more details. • The town of **Fountain** is the self-proclaimed "sinkhole capitol of the U.S." Located 4 miles north of Preston on Highway 52, have a look at one of the sinkholes at a wayside stop.

15 Chatfield

Chatfield is less than 15 miles north of Preston on Highway 52.

Frequently referred to as the "Chosen Valley," Chatfield is home to the International Band Music Lending Library and Pease Wildlife Museum. Several miles west on County 101 is an old stone house where the Jesse James gang once stayed.

Adourn, 218 Main Street South; 507-251-4202. Vintage and antique furniture and accessories. Milk paint and furniture rehab. Open W–Sa. Check website for hours and to sign up for workshops; www.shopadourn.com

Bailiwick, 204 Main Street South; 507-867-3076. General line of antiques and collectibles. Open Th–Sa afternoons.

Just So, 217 Main Street South; 507-993-3149. Antiques, vintage and crafts. Open Tu–Sa.

16 Rochester

Rochester is 20 miles north of Chatfield on Highway 52; 507-288-4331; www.rochestercvb.org or www.visitrochestermn.com

NOTE: See chapter on Rochester (pg. 78) for more things to do.

Churn Dash Antiques, 411 2nd Avenue Northwest (located in Collins Feed & Seed, 2 blocks north of Methodist Hospital); 507-289-4844. Open M–Sa. Furniture, glassware, primitives, toys, kitchen collectibles and more.

John Kruesel's General Merchandise, 22 3rd Street Southwest; 507-289-8049; www.kruesel.com. Open T–Sa. American antiques, early lighting, jewelry, consulting, restoration.

Peterson's Antiques & Stripping, 111 11th Avenue Northeast (11 blocks from downtown); 507-282-9100 or 507-289-0277. Open M–Sa by chance or appointment. Specializing in antique furniture, refinished or as-is. Furniture restoration.

NOTE: You have a choice to make. You can either continue north on Highway 52 into the Twin Cities, or take Highway 14 east to Winona.

17 Highway 52 Route North—Oronoco

From Rochester, take Highway 52 north toward the Twin Cities.

This small town of Oronoco (off of Highway 52) plays host to the annual Gold Rush Days. On the third weekend in August, thousands of folks converge for the huge flea market.

18-21
22-23

Old Rooster Antiques, 106 North Broadway (3 blocks north of Radisson Hotel); 507-287-6228. Open daily. Parking in rear. Multi-dealers featuring stoneware, toys, furniture, clocks, antique doll repair, and more.

Mom's Antique Mall, 1200 Lake Shady Avenue South; 507-367-2600. Over 20 dealers.

18 Pine Island

Pine Island is north of Oronoco on Highway 52.

Lantern Antiques, 512 Main Street South; 507-356-4215. Refinished, painted and "as found" furniture, primitives and accessories. Open M–F year-round and weekends by chance or appointment.

19 Cannon Falls

Cannon Falls is north of Pine Island on Highway 52; www.cannonfalls.org

Country Side Antique Mall, 1161 4th Street South (on the right as you come into town from the south—next to the John Deere dealership); 507-263-0352; www.csamantiques.com. Open daily. Over 50 dealers. Large selection of antiques, collectibles and furniture.

Schaffer's Antiques, 111 North 4th Street (downtown); 507-263-5200. Call for hours. General line, furniture, primitives, tools, pottery, pictures and stoneware.

OPTION

Cannon River Winery, 421 Mill Street West (downtown); 507-263-7400; www.cannonriverwinery.com. If you spot a gorgeous vintage brick building with massive red doors, you've found the charming Cannon River Winery. The winery features about 20 hand-crafted vintages, with reds and whites and a nice apple wine. Stroll through the winery, and partake in a wine tasting. Live music on the weekends. Check website for days and hours.

20 Highway 14 Route West—Eyota

Eyota—if you wish to return to Winona, from Rochester drive east 12 miles on Highway 14.

Eyota Antiques, 30 South Front Street; 507-261-1505; www.eyo taantiques.com. Open F–Su, year-round. Many toys, fat tire bikes, fishing collectibles, signs and advertising and more.

21 St. Charles

St. Charles is east of Eyota on Highway 14. St. Charles City Hall: 507-932-3020

House of Hidden Treasure (1859), 807 Richland Avenue; 507-932-3577. Open May–Nov, daily. Twelve rooms, a garage and a barnful, too. General line. Advertised as "a place where you can dig and lots of dust."

Sarah's Uniques and Jim's "MAN"tiques, 912 Whitewater Avenue; 507-251-0050. Gas pumps and signs, primitives, antiques and collectibles, and much more. Open year-round, W–Su in summer and W–Sa in winter.

Vintage Treasures and Home Décor, 1113 Whitewater Avenue; 507-429-6268. Vintage kitchen, toys, ladies, repurposed furniture, trendy home décor and more.

SW BLUFF COUNTRY ANTIQUING

Not much beats a trip into the beautiful bluff country, unless, of course, it's a trip into the bluff country to hunt antiques.

22 Spring Grove

From the Twin Cities, take Highway 61 south until it turns into I-90 (beyond Winona). Follow I-90 south to Highway 44. Drive southwest on Highway 44 to Spring Grove.

Spring Grove is Minnesota's first Norwegian settlement. Check out their mile-high meringue pie, ten flavors of Spring Grove pop, the Trinity Church carillon and window boxes with rosemaling.

23 Mabel

Mabel is approximately 8 miles west of Spring Grove on Highway 44.

Charles Lindbergh, in his barnstorming days, visited Mabel and gave many of the residents airplane rides. Mabel's Steam Engine Museum displays large steamers, gas engines and threshers.

26
25 24

24 Harmony

Continue west on Highway 44 to Harmony.

Guided Amish tours and cave explorations are a couple of good reasons to visit Harmony. Another is for their antiques!

Slim's Woodshed and Museum, 150 1st Street Northwest; 507-886-3114 or 507-251-0546; www.slimswoodshed.com. Call for hours. You can do it all at Slim's: shop for antiques, reclaimed lumber, take lessons in wood carving and tour the wood carving museum—home of the Caricature Carvers of America Circus. Fee charged for a 1-hour guided tour of museum; free for ages 5 and under.

25 Austin

From Harmony, follow Highway 52 north to Highway 16 west to I-90 west; follow I-90 west into town.

Where does Spam come from? Hormel, of course. Austin is the site of their company headquarters.

Twice As Nice Antiques & Collectibles, 417 North Main Street; 507-433-5353. Open year-round, M–Sa. General line plus furniture.

NOTE: Highway 56 is also the **Shooting Star Scenic Byway**; www.shootingstarbyway.org. The 32-mile, state designated wildflower route is the only place in Minnesota you'll find a wild primrose called the shooting star.

OPTION

Tour the **Spam Museum**, 101 3rd Avenue Northeast; 800-LUV-SPAM (800-588-7726) or 507-437-5641; www.spam.com/museum. Interactive displays and games within 14,000 square feet. Open year-round. Check website for days and hours. Free. • **Jay C. Hormel Nature Center**, 1304 21st Street Northeast; 507-437-7519; www.hormelnaturecenter.org. Once part of the former Hormel estate, explore this beautiful nature center that includes an interpretive building, hiking through woods, gardens, orchards, a pond and streams. Canoe in the summer and cross-country ski in the winter (rentals available for a small fee). Wheelchair-accessible trails. Open daily, year-round; free. • **Mower County Historical Society**, Mower County Fairgrounds, 1303 6th Avenue Southwest; 507-437-6082; www.mowercountyhistory.org. More than 20 buildings house the history of Austin and Mower County. See a steam locomotive, horse-drawn carriages, vintage firefighting equipment, miniature handmade three-ring circus and much more. Open T–F, year-round. Tours available May–Sep. Small fee charged. • **The Old Mill Restaurant**, 3507 11th Place Northeast; 507-437-2076; www.oldmill.net. Built in 1872, the restaurant (once a busy flour mill) overlooks the scenic Cedar River. They offer a full dinner menu, an extensive wine and beer selection, and a long list of to-die-for desserts. Reservations appreciated.

26 Mantorville

Mantorville is on Hwy 57, approximately 40 miles north of Austin.

Memorabilia Antiques, next to Opera House; 507-635-5419. Call for days and hours. General line of antiques, glassware, china, pottery, furniture.

NOTE: See pg. 82 of the Rochester chapter for more information about Mantorville.

Minnehaha Depot

If you love everything about trains, from their screaming whistles to their clacking wheels, then this chapter is for you. Enjoy all the train rides, museums, depots, toys, restaurants and streetcars in the pages ahead, but save some time for exploring the many interesting area attractions included in the options.

TRAINS, TRAINS & MORE TRAINS

MISSISSIPPI TRAIN TRACKING
Caribou Coffee, *Red Wing* 112

Red Wing Visitors and Convention Bureau, *Red Wing* 112

Levee Park, *Red Wing* 112
Options: Bay Point Park, Boathouse Village, Memorial Park, Barn Bluff, Falconer Vineyards, Flower Valley Vineyard

Lock and Dam No. 4, *Alma, WI* 113
Option: Buena Vista Park

STREETCAR DESIRE
Jackson Street Roundhouse, *St. Paul* 114

Minnehaha Depot, *Minneapolis* 114

Como-Harriet Streetcar Line, *Minneapolis* 114

Excelsior Streetcar Line, *Minneapolis* 115

THE ROMANTIC ERA
Historic 1916 Osceola Depot, *Osceola, WI* 115
Option: Cascade Falls

Union Depot, *St. Paul* 116

WHISTLE STOP
Whistle Stop Inn Bed & Breakfast, *New York Mills* 116
Options: New York Mills Regional Cultural Center, Great American Think-Off, World's Largest Art Tractor, Finn Creek Open Air Museum

1-4

MISSISSIPPI TRAIN TRACKING

These attractions follow the rail tracks along the Mississippi River from Red Wing, MN, to Alma, WI. From the Twin Cities, take Highway 61 south to Red Wing (about 50 miles).

1 Caribou Coffee

726 Main Street, Red Wing, MN; 651-388-1910; www.cariboucoffee.com

For anyone into trains, this is one coffeehouse you're going to want to see. Built at the turn of the twentieth century, there's a real sense of déja vu as you stand in line to place an order. It's not hard to imagine a bustling depot of travelers standing in line to purchase tickets. The two-story red brick building has customer seating on both levels. Wheelchair accessible.

2 Red Wing Visitors and Convention Bureau

420 Levee Street (behind the St. James Hotel), Red Wing, MN; 651-385-5934; www.redwing.org

Located in the historic depot (building listed on the National Register of Historic Places), the friendly staff at the Red Wing Visitors and Convention Bureau can hook you up with anything from fishing guides to upcoming city events. Check out all the wonderful train memorabilia. Open M–F.

3 Levee Park

Bush and Levee Streets (behind the St. James Hotel), Red Wing, MN

The Levee Park vantage offers front row viewing of the Red Wing Grain Company cargo train loading operation.

OPTION

Although this has nothing to do with trains, follow Levee Street west to **Bay Point Park**. Marvel at the skill required of tug captains as they maneuver barges through one of the sharpest turns on the Mississippi River. The park is also home

to the **Boathouse Village**, a rare remaining example of a "gin pole" system. The system allows boathouses to adjust to the different water levels by riding up and down on poles.
• Get a sweeping view of Red Wing from **Memorial Park**, especially breathtaking during the fall "leaf season." Take East 7th Street to Skyline Drive • **Barn Bluff** is a favorite spot for hikers and cliff climbers. There are two trails leading to the top: the front trail with concrete steps and the more difficult riverside hike through the woods. Take East 5th Street pass under Highway 61. Trail begins on left side. Free.
• **Falconer Vineyards**, 3572 Old Tyler Road; 651-388-8849; www.falconervineyards.com. Open year-round. Check website for days and hours. You'll enjoy the beautiful river valley scenery as well as the wines. Pack a picnic basket and soak in the view. Small fee charged for wine sampling. **Flower Valley Vineyard**, 29212 Orchard Road; 651-388-1770; flowervalleyvineyard.com. A beautiful farm setting and a barn from 1873 are the perfect backdrop to enjoy the vineyard's wines, which grow from winter-hardy grapes located on-site.

4 Lock and Dam No. 4

Alma, WI. Observation deck on Highway 35 (16 miles from Pepin).

You're probably wondering what a lock and dam is doing on a train tour. To get to the observation deck, you first have to cross the train tracks—accomplished via an open catwalk. Stop midway on the catwalk while a train rushes directly below your feet. There's nothing quite as exhilarating (or terrifying!) as experiencing these mighty beasts from point-blank range. You won't have to wait long for a train, as more than 50 pass this spot daily. Free.

OPTION

While in Alma, venture 500 feet uphill to **Buena Vista Park**. *Better Homes and Gardens* magazine referred to the view as "one of the river valley's finest natural balconies." Take Highway E and follow signs; 2½ miles. Open year-round. Picnic tables, scenic overlook, hiking trail. Free.

NOTE: For more about Alma, see pg. 99.

STREETCAR DESIRE

This fun day begins in St. Paul for a tour of the state's first locomotive repair shop and ends with a ride on one of the oldest operating museum-quality trolleys in the country.

5 Jackson Street Roundhouse

193 East Pennsylvania Avenue, St. Paul; 651-228-0263. www.transportationmuseum.org

Built in 1862 by the Minnesota and Pacific Railroad, the Jackson Street Roundhouse stands on the site of Minnesota's first locomotive repair shop. James J. Hill, founder of the Great Northern Railway, rebuilt the structure to its present form in 1907. The Jackson Street Roundhouse closed in 1960.

The grounds feature historical railroad equipment and an interpretive center. Fascinating exhibits bring alive the sights and sounds of the golden railroad era. Open W & Sa, year-round. Check website for hours and special events. Wheelchair accessible. Fee charged.

6 Minnehaha Depot

4926 Minnehaha Avenue in Minnehaha Park, Minneapolis; 651-228-0263; www.transportationmuseum.org

Delicate gingerbread architecture earned the Minnehaha Depot a title of "Princess." The 1875 depot served as a freight station until 1963 and is now owned by the Minnesota Historical Society. Step inside and listen to train sounds from the 1920s or operate the telegraph key. Open Memorial Day–Labor Day on Sundays. Free.

7 Como-Harriet Streetcar Line

Board streetcars at the Linden Hills Station, 4200 Queen Avenue South, Minneapolis; 952-922-1096; www.trolleyride.org

Enjoy a trip back to the 1900s aboard the antique, century-old streetcars. A 2-mile, 15-minute ride costs $2.00 and is worth every cent; free for children 3 and under. Visit the station exhibits and museum store or take a leisurely walk around the lake. Open May–Oct. Check website for days and hours.

8 Excelsior Streetcar Line

From Minneapolis, take Highway 7 to the Excelsior exit to Water Street. The platform is on the left; 952-922-1096; www.trolleyride.org

Take Highway 7 west past the Excelsior exit to County Road 19. Turn right at County 19 and right again at Water Street. The station is between 3rd and George Streets on the right. Catch the streetcar May–Oct. Check website for days and hours. Fee charged, free for children 3 and under.

NOTE: For more ideas on what to do while in Excelsior, see the section in the Romantic Getaways chapter on pg. 86.

THE ROMANTIC ERA

These attractions are for romantics and train lovers alike. Begin in St. Paul with lunch at the Union Depot, and then take an hour-long scenic drive northeast to Osceola, WI, where you will board a vintage train for a leisurely ride.

9 Historic 1916 Osceola Depot

114 Depot Road, Osceola, WI; 715-755-3570 or 651-228-0263; www.transportationmuseum.org

Begin your vintage rail experience with the purchase of a ticket at the fully restored 1916 Soo Line Depot. Constructed of wire-cut red brick and white sandstone, the depot was a marvel in its day, featuring both mens' and ladies' indoor toilets.

The Osceola & St. Croix Valley Railway offers round-trips aboard diesel powered trains. The westbound 90-minute trip traverses steep rock cliffs and an untamed river valley, while the shorter, 50-minute eastbound trip passes through miles of picturesque Wisconsin dairyland. Special scheduled trips include Fireworks Express, William O'Brien Naturalist Trip, Fall Leaf Watchers' Trip and more (some include meals). Call or check website for dates and ticket prices. Gift shop in depot; store on the train. Open Sa–Su, May–Oct. Fee charged.

OPTION

Loaded with Midwestern friendliness and old-fashioned charm, there's more to do in Osceola than ride trains. Stretch the legs with a hike down a winding stairway (131 steps) to beautiful **Cascade Falls**, conveniently located on Cascade Street, Osceola's main drag.

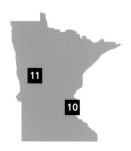

10 Union Depot

214 East 4th Street, downtown St. Paul; www.uniondepot.org

This once-bustling 1917 train station is absolutely breathtaking with its elegant interior of massive marble pillars, granite floors and beautiful ironwork. It is also home to Christos Greek Restaurant; 651-224-6000; www.christos.com.

WHISTLE STOP

New York Mills is 30 miles southeast of Detroit Lakes on Highway 10 between Perham and Wadena.

11 Whistle Stop Inn Bed & Breakfast

New York Mills, 1 block south, then 1 block east of 4-way stop; 800-328-6315 or 218-385-2223; www.whistlestopbedandbreakfast.com

All aboard! This is one of the quietest train trips you'll ever take, because not one of the five railroad cars ever goes anywhere. Whistle Stop innkeepers Jann and Roger Lee offer a truly unique experience: plush overnight accommodations in elegant vintage railroad cars. Two cars feature double whirlpools, fireplaces and sitting rooms; another showcases an antique claw-foot tub. All include in-room coffee and tea service and full breakfast. Open year-round.

Accommodations at the Whistle Stop Inn are also available in the gorgeous 1903 Victorian home. Oak woodwork, antiques and railroad memorabilia.

NOTE: New York Mills, a town of 1,000, was named one of the top five culturally cool towns by *USA Weekend* magazine. Located about 170 miles from the Twin Cities, it's only one hour away from Itasca State Park. See the Harley Trip in the Extreme Adventures chapter on pg. 29 for more things to do.

OPTION

New York Mills Regional Cultural Center, 24 North Main Avenue; 218-385-3339; www.kulcher.org. The center features musical performances, gallery exhibits, summer art classes, an artists' retreat program and the annual **Great American Think-Off**. Hosted on the Sunday before Father's Day, the Think-Off draws essay contestants from around the world, ranging from a 15-year-old cheerleader to a priest from New York. An online C-SPAN audience, as well as the theater audience, vote on the winner. A past debate topic posed: The Nature of Humanity: Inherently Good or Inherently Evil? Oddly enough, the debate ended in a tie. • See the **World's Largest Art Tractor** in Sculpture Park, New York Mills. • **Finn Creek Open Air Museum**; 218-385-2233. Tour the restored 18-acre farm established in 1900 by Finnish immigrants Siffert and Wilhelmina Tapio. Original house and sauna, blacksmith shop and barns. Open Memorial Day–Labor Day, Th–Su. Located 3 miles east of New York Mills on Highway 10, south 2.5 miles on Highway 106, then a half mile west on a gravel road.

Cascade River State Park

If you're crazy about waterfalls, this chapter will put you over the edge. The North Shore Scenic Drive alone includes more than 20 falls, and that's not counting the ones tumbling from the rocks along the highway!

WATERFALLS

FOLLOW THE FALLS

St. Anthony Falls, *Minneapolis* 120
Option: Mill City Museum

Minnehaha Falls, *Minneapolis* 121
Option: Minnehaha Depot

Vermillion Falls, *Hastings* 121
Option: Historic Hastings

Cannon Falls. 121
Option: Cannon Valley Trail

Zumbrota 122

AMNICON & PATTISON STATE PARKS

Amnicon Falls State Park, *Superior, WI* 122
Option: Wisconsin Point

Pattison State Park, *Superior, WI* 123

NORTH SHORE SCENIC DRIVE

Option: Lake Superior Maritime Visitor Center

Gooseberry Falls State Park, *Two Harbors* 123
Options: Split Rock Lighthouse, Minnesota's only operating light station,
3M Sandpaper Museum, Superior Hiking Trail

Tettegouche State Park, *Silver Bay* 124
Options: Palisade Head, Caribou Falls Wayside, Cross River Falls

Temperance River State Park, *Schroeder* 125
Option: Lutsen Mountains

Cascade River State Park, *Lutsen* 125
Option: Gunflint Trail

Judge C. R. Magney State Park, *Grand Marais* 125
Option: Naniboujou Lodge & Restaurant

Grand Portage State Park, *Grand Portage* 126
Options: Grand Portage National Monument, Isle Royale National Park

FOLLOW THE FALLS

Explore several waterfalls and Minnesota's last remaining covered bridge—all within a comfortable hour's drive of the Twin Cities.

1 St. Anthony Falls

St. Anthony Falls Historic District, on the Mississippi River between Plymouth Avenue North and the I-35W bridge in Minneapolis.

St. Anthony Falls holds the honored distinction of being the only waterfall on the Mississippi River. The falls are only 13 feet, but the actual drop is around 50 feet, making it the longest drop on the river as well.

View the falls from the restored Stone Arch Bridge and explore the nineteenth-century Nicollet Island neighborhood. Tour the industrial ruins of the Minneapolis flour milling district, once the largest in the world. Trail open year-round. Group guided walking tours offered for a fee; 612-341-7556; www.millcitymuseum.org.

OPTION

As long as you're in the area, check out the **Mill City Museum**, 704 South 2nd Street, Minneapolis; 612-341-7555; www.millcitymuseum.org. The museum is built within the charred ruins of what was once the world's largest flour mill and showcases many original features, such as the flour bins, engine house, some of the milling machinery, and a wheat house. Step inside a 15-foot box of Bisquick and watch TV commercials from the past. Sample homemade bread in the Baking Lab. Ride the Flour Tower, an eight-story elevator ride that highlights the mill's history. Open year-round, the museum features hands-on activities, and a gift shop. Fee charged. But there's so much more to do in this historic falls district: carriage rides, trolley rides, free concerts, Water Power Park, Nicollet Island, Mill Ruins Park, St. Anthony Main, to name a few. Check out the website, www.stanthonymain.com, for a quick overall of events, restaurants, tour sites, and more.

2 Minnehaha Falls

Inside Minnehaha Park off of Minnehaha Parkway, Minneapolis.

An awesome sight of rushing water over a limestone ledge, but during a dry season Minnehaha Falls isn't much more than a dribble. A convenient stairway leads to a closer view.

OPTION

While here, be sure to visit the **Minnehaha Depot**. Operate the telegraph key and listen to train sounds from the 1920s; 651-228-0263; www.transportationmuseum.org. Open Memorial Day–Labor Day on Sundays. Free.

3 Vermillion Falls

Hastings, follow Highway 55, turn south onto Highway 61, turn left on 21st Street East by the Ardent Mills (immediately after County 47 junction).

Probably the best kept secret the enchanting river town of Hastings has is the Vermillion Falls. Against a backdrop of old limestone, the 50-foot-wide, 19-foot-high falls make an ideal place for a picnic. So spread the checkered cloth and pass around the chicken salad while enjoying a picture-perfect view.

NOTE: About a half mile below the falls are the remains of the state's first flour mill, built in 1857. The mill is the oldest continuing flour milling operation in Minnesota. Follow trail.

OPTION

Historic Hastings has a well-preserved downtown district with fine dining, antique shops and specialty stores. For more information, contact the Hastings Area Chamber of Commerce and Tourism Bureau, 314 Vermillion Street, Suite 100, Hastings; 651-437-6775; www.hastingsmn.org.

4 Cannon Falls

Cannon Falls, take Highway 61 south to County 20. Follow signs.

In actuality, Cannon Falls is a man-made dam, recently reduced to a bump, but still worth the trip. Look for it on the right side as you enter town from the north. Enjoy the park's resident swans and ducks. Stroll the main drag, with its bakery, yarn shop and quaint gift and antique stores. Cannon Falls is a real find for those folks needing a relaxing day away from it all.

OPTION

The 20-mile, paved **Cannon Valley Trail** (former Chicago Great Western Railroad line) runs along the Cannon River from Cannon Falls to Red Wing. Very scenic trail used by hikers, bikers and cross-country skiers.

5 Zumbrota

Zumbrota is a short 20-mile trip south of Cannon Falls on Highway 52; zumbrotacoveredbridge.com

It's not your imagination—the towns really are getting smaller, but ever larger on charm and scenery. Zumbrota is a mix of rolling farmland and river country. No waterfall, but it is the proud home of Minnesota's last remaining covered bridge—and it's painted red, too! Located very near its original site, the 1869 bridge was the main stagecoach route between Iowa and St. Paul. Where can you find this magnificent marvel? Where else but in Covered Bridge Park. Look for it on the edge of town heading northeast on Highway 58.

AMNICON & PATTISON STATE PARKS

Located on the western tip of Wisconsin, Amnicon and Pattison State Parks feature many spectacular waterfalls, and they're only a short drive from Duluth (150 miles from the Twin Cities). The entries below "follow the falls" north.

6 Amnicon Falls State Park

10 miles southeast of Superior, WI, on Highway 2. Follow signs; 715-398-3000

Amnicon Falls State Park has one of the most beautiful series of cascades and waterfalls in the Midwest. At the heart of the park, the Amnicon River separates, forming two streams. Three water-falls plunge nearly 30 feet each. During good water flow, the river fills another channel producing a fourth falls. A rare, 55-foot Horton bowstring bridge spans the river, giving access to an island. Only five other Horton bridges are known to exist. The view of the Lower Falls is wheelchair accessible. Open year-round. Park permit required.

OPTION

Sorry, no waterfalls at **Wisconsin Point**, just an unforget-tably spectacular view of Lake Superior. Miles of sandy beach, lighthouse (not open for tours), Indian cemetery and an excellent place to hunt agates. Located on the outskirts of Superior, WI. From Superior, take East 2nd Street to Moccasin Mike Road. Turn north onto Wisconsin Point Road.

7 Pattison State Park

Located 13 miles south of Superior, WI, on Highway 35, or 20 miles southwest of Amnicon Falls State Park. From Amnicon, retrace your route on Highway 2 (north toward Superior) to County Z (west), take County A south to County B, follow signs; 715-399-3111

At 165 dizzying feet high, Big Manitou Falls is the highest waterfall in Wisconsin. One mile farther south (on Highway 35), Little Manitou Falls measures in with a drop of 31 feet. Pattison State Park is also the site of a 1930s Civilian Conservation Corps camp. Nature center, hiking trails, geology walk, camping, fishing, swimming beach and bathhouse, picnic facilities. Winter activities include cross-country ski trails, snowshoeing, hiking and ice skating. Open year-round. Wheelchair accessible. Park permit required.

NORTH SHORE SCENIC DRIVE

From Duluth, head north on Scenic Highway 61 to the Canadian border (about 150 miles).

Each year, the North Shore Scenic Drive—Minnesota's most romantic tour of the Lake Superior shoreline—draws visitors by the millions. One trip around this block and you'll know why.

NOTE: Minnesota state parks require vehicle permits. Information about purchasing permits is available at the DNR website; www.dnr.state.mn.us/state_parks/permit.html.

OPTION

Lake Superior, the largest of the five Great Lakes, holds ten percent of the world's fresh water—the average temperature is 40 °F. It is breathtaking and deadly, having claimed hundreds of ships over the years. A good place to start any exploration of the North Shore is the **Lake Superior Maritime Visitor Center**. It provides a history of the lake and features full-sized replicas of ship cabins, an operating steam engine, film presentations and more. Located on the waterfront in Canal Park next to the Aerial Lift Bridge; 218-720-5260, ext. 1; www.lsmma.com. Open year-round. Wheelchair accessible. Free.

8 Gooseberry Falls State Park

3206 Highway 61, Two Harbors; 218-595-7100; www.dnr.state.mn.us/state_parks/gooseberry_falls/index.html

Gooseberry Falls State Park receives nearly a million visitors annually. It features five waterfalls with 18 miles of picturesque hiking trails. The interior trails cross the Gooseberry River several times via footbridges.

The visitor center includes a rest stop, a nature store, an interpretive center and maps of the trails. Open year-round. Those who use the park as a rest stop need not buy a permit. Wheelchair accessible.

OPTION

Although you won't see any waterfalls, a stop at **Split Rock Lighthouse** is a must. Built in 1910, the lighthouse commands a magnificent view of Lake Superior from atop a 130-foot cliff. Tour of the lighthouse, fog-signal building and keeper's home conducted daily mid-May through mid-Oct. The history center is open Th–M during some winter months. Check website for days and hours; 218-226-6372; sites.mnhs.org/ historic-sites/split-rock-lighthouse. Museum store, interactive history center, movie. Fee charged. • Take a guided tour of **Minnesota's only operating light station** (also a B&B!), 1 Lighthouse Point, Two Harbors; 888-832-5606; www. lighthousebb.org (about 30 miles north of Duluth on Highway 61). Fee charged. • Built in 1898, tour Minnesota Mining and Manufacturing's (3M's) first office building, now the only **sandpaper museum** in the world. Hands-on interactive programs; 2nd Avenue and Waterfront Drive, Two Harbors. Lake County Historical Society; 218-834-4898; www.lakecounty-historicalsociety.org. Fee charged. • Highway 61 offers many access points for the **Superior Hiking Trail**, named one of the world's top 25 trails. Three hundred miles of rugged and challenging territory; 218-834-2700; www.shta.org.

9 Tettegouche State Park

5702 Highway 61, Silver Bay; 218-226-6365;
www.dnr.state.mn.us/state_parks/tettegouche/index.html

The Baptism River flows through Tettegouche State Park creating three waterfalls, including the spectacular 60-foot High Falls. Hike to the historic logging camp on Mic Mac Lake, or better still, rent one of the no-frills rustic cabins. Twenty-three miles of trails. Visitor center with exhibits open year-round.

OPTION

Get a sweeping view of Lake Superior from the 350-foot-high **Palisade Head**. Cliffs have colorful red outcrops. Overlook is on the right side of Highway 61, directly before

Tettegouche State Park entrance. Watch for sign. • **Caribou Falls Wayside** is 12 miles farther north on the left side of Highway 61. Stretch the legs with a short, very scenic hike to the falls (less than a mile). Rugged trail. • Continuing north on Highway 61, view the **Cross River Falls** and gorge from the highway bridge in Schroeder.

10 Temperance River State Park

7620 Highway 61 East, P.O. Box 33, Schroeder; 218-663-7476;
www.dnr.state.mn.us/state_parks/temperance_river/index.html

Within the park, the Temperance River drops 162 feet in a half-mile series of cascades, creating cauldrons and giant potholes. Hidden Falls is upriver from the parking area along Highway 61. Twenty-two miles of trails.

OPTION

Lutsen Mountains offers a 2-mile, 8-passenger gondola ride with a breathtaking view of Lake Superior and surrounding mountain ridges. Off of Highway 61, Lutsen; 218-663-7281; www.lutsen.com.

11 Cascade River State Park

3481 Highway 61 West, Lutsen; 218-387-3053;
www.dnr.state.mn.us/state_parks/cascade_river/index.html

Numerous waterfalls are created by the Cascade River as it twists through a rocky gorge, dropping 225 feet in one mile. Fifteen miles of gorgeous trails. Open year-round.

OPTION

The **Gunflint Trail** begins at scenic Grand Marais. Have a pizza topped with wild rice and sauerkraut (or whatever your taste buds desire) at the famous Sven and Ole's, located at 9 West Wisconsin Street. Stroll out to the Grand Marais lighthouse and watch the waves crash against the breakers.

12 Judge C. R. Magney State Park

4051 Highway 61, Grand Marais; 218-387-3039;
www.dnr.state.mn.us/state_parks/judge_cr_magney/index.html

Set out along the Brule River trail in Judge C. R. Magney State Park to hunt for agates and waterfalls. The Brule divides around a large boulder—one side falls 50 feet into a pool below, while the other plunges into a pothole known as the Devil's Kettle and is never seen again. Three waterfalls and nine miles of trails.

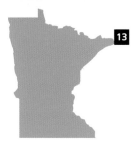

OPTION

Built in 1929 along the shoreline of Lake Superior, **Naniboujou Lodge's** original owners intended it as an exclusive club for the wealthy; Babe Ruth, Ring Lardner and Jack Dempsey were among its charter members. However, the stock market crash lead to its mortgage foreclosure and sale. After changing many hands, the lodge underwent a restoration and is on the National Register of Historic Places. Retaining its original Cree Indian design, the Naniboujou Great Hall serves as the restaurant's dining room. The fireplace consists of 200 tons of stone gathered from the beach, making it one of Minnesota's tallest native-stone fireplaces. There are 24 guest rooms, five have wood-burning fireplaces. Delicious meals prepared in their excellent restaurant. Afternoon teas served in the solarium/library. Gift shop. Box lunches available for hikers. Open mid-May through Oct and some weekends during winter season (check website); 218-387-2688; www.naniboujou.com.

13 Grand Portage State Park

9393 Highway 61 West, Grand Portage; 218-475-2360
www.dnr.state.mn.us/state_parks/grand_portage/index.html

About as close to the Canadian border as a Minnesotan can get, Grand Portage State Park features two waterfalls. A half-mile hike leads to the incredible 120-foot High Falls on the Pigeon River (wheelchair accessible). Another 2.5-mile trail takes you to Middle Falls.

OPTION

Established in 1731, Grand Portage was Minnesota's first white settlement. Costumed interpreters at the **Grand Portage National Monument** demonstrate birch bark canoe making, adobe oven bread baking and all sorts of other eighteenth-century crafts. Off Highway 61 in Grand Portage. Watch for signs; 218-475-0123; www.nps.gov/grpo. Fee charged. • Spend a day fishing and exploring or camp the weekend on **Isle Royale National Park**. The only way to get there is by boat. Grand Portage Isle Royale Transportation Line, Inc.; 218-475-0024; www.grand-isle-royale.com.

Minnehaha Falls

They say there's nothing better for quenching a powerful thirst than water, but then again the folks who say that probably never had one of Minnesota's home-brewed ales in a frosty mug.

Many of the state's award-winning wines began as winter-hardy grapes. Tour the breweries and vineyards in this chapter, then taste their offerings and you'll know why Minnesota is a winner in both industries.

WINE & BEER LOVERS' TOURS

ALEXANDRIA
Carlos Creek Winery, *Alexandria* 130
Options: Kensington Runestone Museum, Big Ole, Inspiration Peak, Phelps Mill,
Home of Sinclair Lewis

SOUTHERN MINNESOTA TASTINGS
August Schell Brewery, *New Ulm* 131

Morgan Creek Vineyards, *New Ulm* 131
Option: New Ulm Glockenspiel

The Wine Cafe Pub & Eatery, *Mankato* 131
Options: Minneopa State Park, Sibley Park, Mankato Mdewakanton Powwow,
Mount Kato Ski Area, Minnesota Vikings practice, Performing arts

ST. CROIX VALLEY
Saint Croix Vineyards, *Stillwater*. 133

Northern Vineyards, *Stillwater* 133
Option: Gasthaus Bavarian Hunter Restaurant

Alexis Bailly Vineyard, *Hastings* 133

TWIN CITIES BREWERIES
Summit Brewing, *St. Paul*. 134

Vine Park Brewing, *St. Paul* 134

ALEXANDRIA

To get to Alexandria, take I-94 west of the Twin Cities (120 miles).

1 Carlos Creek Winery

6693 County 34 Northwest; 320- 846-5443; www.carloscreekwinery.com

Located on 160 acres, there is plenty for kids and grown-ups to do, and lots of room to roam at Carlos Creek Winery. Award-winning wines from their 20-acre vineyard are fermented and bottled on the property. Open year-round. Daily tours and wine tasting. Fall grape-stomping contest.

OPTION

Alexandria considers itself to be the "birthplace of America," claiming the Vikings explored Minnesota long before Columbus made his voyage. The proof is in the Runestone—a rock found in a nearby field, allegedly dating to 1362 and inscribed by Vikings. See the famous stone, the tooth of a woolly mammoth and much more at the **Kensington Runestone Museum,** 206 Broadway; 320-763-3160; www.runestonemuseum.org. Check website for hours. Fee charged. • Have your picture taken with **Big Ole**, the 28-foot, 4-ton Viking greeter as you enter town. • **Inspiration Peak**, off County 5, north of nearby Brandon. Panoramic views from 1,750 feet—the highest point in western Minnesota. • Explore the 1889 **Phelps Mill**, one of the most photographed sites in the state. Park includes a flour mill, millpond and stream— a great spot for a picnic or relaxing with a book. Fifteen miles east of Fergus Falls off Highway 1; 218-826-6159. • Visit the boyhood home of Nobel Prize novelist **Sinclair Lewis**. The gray clapboard building retains much of the Lewis family furniture; 810 Sinclair Lewis Avenue, Sauk Center (near downtown); 320-352-5201. Open T–Sa, Memorial Day–Labor Day. Fee charged.

SOUTHERN MINNESOTA TASTINGS

New Ulm is approximately 90 miles from the Twin Cities. Follow Highway 169 south to St. Peter; take County 99 to Nicollet; then Highway 14 west.

2 August Schell Brewery

1860 Schell Road, New Ulm. South on Broadway, turn west on 18th Street South, follow the signs; 507-354-5528 or 800-770-5020; www.schellsbrewery.com

Where can you go to get a good Wiener Schnitzel and a hearty German beer to wash it down with? New Ulm, of course.

The August Schell Brewery opened in 1860. Currently operated by the fifth generation, Schell's is the second-oldest family-owned brewery in the nation. Grounds include a deer park and beautiful gardens, and also the outdoor "Biergarten" (beer garden) on summer weekends. Brewery tours offered Memorial Day–Labor Day, daily; Labor Day–Memorial Day, F–Su. Small fee charged. Grounds and museum/gift shop open daily. Free.

3 Morgan Creek Vineyards

23707 478th Avenue, New Ulm. From New Ulm, take Highway 68 roughly 10 miles east toward Mankato; watch for sign. Turn right on County 47, go for 2 miles, take left on County 101. First place on left. Use second entrance; 507-947-3547; www.morgancreekvineyards.com

Maybe you're not as German as you'd like to be and find beer a bit too robust for the palate? Then take a trip to Morgan Creek Vineyards for some wine instead. Seasonal events for the entire family include a Grape Stomp Festival the first Saturday in October. Tours and tastings Apr–Dec. Check website for days and hours.

OPTION

While you're in town, be sure to see the **New Ulm Glockenspiel**. Time your visit to the freestanding carillon clock tower for noon, 3 p.m. or 5 p.m. and watch animated figures move to the programmed music of the bells. Located downtown on the corner of Minnesota Street and North 4th. For more information about New Ulm, call 888-4NEWULM (888-463-9856) or visit their website at www.newulm.com.

4 The Wine Cafe Pub & Eatery

301 North Riverfront, Mankato; 507-345-1516; www.winecafebar.com

Driving eastward on Highway 14 to Mankato, the Wine Cafe Pub & Eatery serves over 100 wines by the glass, as well as a very large beer selection. Open daily.

**5-6
7**

OPTION

Mankato has more than 30 parks, offering anything from fishing to mountain biking; www.mankatomn.gov. But for the romantic, stop in at **Minneopa State Park**. This park has a picturesque double waterfall and an old windmill that was built in 1864. Located 5 miles west of Mankato near the junction of Highways 68 & 169. Follow signs; 507-389-5464; www.dnr.state.mn.us/state_parks/minneo pa/index.html. State Park permit required. • A free petting zoo, flower gardens and a fountain are a few of the things you'll see at **Sibley Park**. Come in the winter for sledding and ice skating; 900 Mound Avenue. • **Mankato Mdewakanton Powwow**—American Indians from across the country return to their ceremonial grounds in Land of Memories Park. Colorful costumes, traditional foods, crafts and ceremonial dancing. Mid-Sep. Park located across the river from Sibley Park. Call the Mankato Area Chamber & Convention Bureau for more information; 800-697-0652 or 507-385-6640; www.greatermankato.com. • **Mount Kato Ski Area** has 19 trails, 8 chairlifts, a 2-level chalet, full-service rental shop and more. Also 7 miles of mountain bike trails—80 percent is wooded single track. Located 1 mile south of Mankato. Take Highway 66 south. Follow signs; 507-625-3363; www.mountkato.com. • Mid-July to mid-August, watch the **Minnesota Vikings** get in shape for the upcoming season at their Mankato training camp. Minnesota State University, Blakeslee Field. Practices held twice a day, 6 days a week. Free. Fee charged for scrimmages; www.vikings.com • Mankato also has an extensive **performing arts** theater schedule. Call the Mankato Area Chamber & Convention Bureau; 800-697-0652 or 507-385-6640; www.mankatomn.gov or www.greatermankato.com.

ST. CROIX VALLEY

These attractions begin in Stillwater and end just a few miles south of Hastings. From the Twin Cities, take a 20-minute drive east on I-94 to Highway 95 north into Stillwater. Another option is Highway 36 east.

5 Saint Croix Vineyards

6428 Manning Avenue North, Stillwater; 651-430-3310; www.scvwines.com

Minnesota's winter-hardy grapes produce award-winning wines. The Saint Croix Vineyards, located at Aamodt's Apple Farm, is 3 miles west of Stillwater on Manning Avenue off of Highway 36. Sample their Raspberry Infusion, Frontenac, or any of their other vintages offered at the on-site tasting room/winery. See if you don't agree that Minnesota knows good wine. Open mid-Feb to Dec. Check website for days and hours.

NOTE: Aamodt's also provides hot air balloon rides for a fee. See more on pg. 87.

6 Northern Vineyards

223 North Main Street, Stillwater; 651-430-1032; www.northernvineyards.com

Visit Northern Vineyards' winery and tasting room. This cooperative is owned and operated by the Minnesota Wine Growers. It produces a wide selection of local wines. Tours are by appointment. Open daily.

OPTION

Don't worry, beer lovers, you haven't been forgotten. The **Gasthaus Bavarian Hunter Restaurant** serves award-winning German cuisine and imported beer from Munich. And for a special treat, stop in on a Friday evening or Sunday afternoon for toe-tapping, live accordion music. Open daily; 8390 Lofton Avenue, Stillwater; 651-439-7128; www.gast-hausbavarianhunter.com.

NOTE: For more things to do in Stillwater, see the Romantic Getaways chapter on pg. 84.

7 Alexis Bailly Vineyard

18200 Kirby Avenue, Hastings; 651-437-1413; www.abvwines.com

Alexis Bailly Vineyard produces nine wines with a label that reads, "Minnesota: Where the grapes can suffer." Tastings of their acclaimed wines are offered Jun–Nov, F–Su.

NOTE: For more to do in Hastings, see Waterfalls chapter, pg. 118.

8-9

TWIN CITIES BREWERIES

8 Summit Brewing

910 Montreal Circle, St. Paul; 651-265-7800; www.summitbrewing.com

Established in 1986, Summit Brewing began life in an old auto parts warehouse and grew into a brand new facility in 1998. And no matter what fine Minnesota watering hole you saunter into, you're going to find yourself face-to-face with a Summit beer. So go ahead, order a round and you'll see why this brewery's beverage is a staple on the beer list. As founder Mark Stutrud says, "We only brew what we love to drink. Whatever's left over, we sell." Summit's Beer Hall & Tap Room is open Th–Sa, with food trucks on-site and special events and entertainment. Free brewery tours are available T–Sa. Check website for details, days and hours and to make tour reservations.

9 Vine Park Brewing

1254 West 7th Street, St. Paul; 651-228-1355; www.vinepark.com

Vine Park is the state's only Brew-On-Premise (BOP) brewery and as a 20-year-old site, it is also one of the oldest and most successful BOPs in the nation. All good news for those do-it-yourself brew masters who don't want the fuss, muss, and expense involved with home brewing. Vine Park Brewing provides the recipes, the ingredients, the equipment, the knowledge, and the beer coach. You provide yourself, about two hours of time, and the fee it takes to brew one batch of beer which yields about seventy-two 22-oz. bottles (plus a bottle deposit). This is a great hands-on opportunity to create your own special ale. Reservations taken T–Sa.

NOTE: Winemaking also available. Vine Park is not an eatery or bar.

Target Field, Minneapolis

The Odds & Ends chapter includes tons of useful information not available through the theme chapters. Use the map above as a quick reference for pinpointing Minnesota's beautiful Scenic Byways.

When you think "Minnesota," think perfect powder hills for downhill skiing, professional sports, renowned theater, and great music. The Odds & Ends chapter showcases a wide selection of these venues.

ODDS & ENDS

HAUNTED MINNESOTA

Fitzgerald Theater, *St. Paul*. 140

Forepaugh's Restaurant, *St. Paul* 140

Guthrie Theater, *Minneapolis*. 140

Minneapolis City Hall, *Minneapolis* 140

Ramsey County Courthouse, *St. Paul*. 140

St. John's University, *Collegeville*. 141

St. Mary's College, *Winona*. 141

The Palace Theatre, *Luverne* 141

MINNESOTA'S FORGOTTEN FOREST

The Lost Forty 141
> Option: Hafeman Boat Works

SCENIC BYWAYS

Apple Blossom Drive 142

Avenue of Pines 142

Edge of the Wilderness. 142

Glacial Ridge Trail. 142

Grand Rounds 143

Great River Road 143

Gunflint Trail 143

Historic Bluff Country. 143

Lady Slipper 143

Lake Country 144

Minnesota River Valley. 144

North Shore 144

Otter Trail. 144

Paul Bunyan 144

Rushing Rapids. 145

Shooting Star 145

Skyline Parkway 145

Veterans Evergreen Memorial. 145

Waters of the Dancing Sky 145

SPORTS
Canterbury Park (Horse Racing), *Shakopee* 146

Minnesota Lynx WNBA Basketball, *Minneapolis* 146

Minnesota Timberwolves Basketball, *Minneapolis*. 146

Minnesota Twins Baseball, *Minneapolis* 146

Minnesota Vikings Football, *Minneapolis*. 146

Minnesota Wild NHL Hockey, *St. Paul* 146

Running Aces Harness Park (Horse Racing), *Columbus* 146

St. Paul Saints Baseball, *St. Paul* 146

University of Minnesota Athletics, *Minneapolis* 146

TWIN CITIES THEATER & MUSIC
Brave New Workshop, *Minneapolis* 147

Chanhassen Dinner Theatres, *Chanhassen* 147

Children's Theatre Company, *Minneapolis*. 147

Fitzgerald Theater, *St. Paul*. 147

Guthrie Theater, *Minneapolis*. 147

Historic State and Orpheum Theatres, *Minneapolis* 147

History Theatre, *St. Paul* 147

Orchestra Hall, *Minneapolis* 148

Ordway Music Theatre, *St. Paul* 148

Park Square Theatre Company, *St. Paul*. 148

Penumbra Theatre Company, *St. Paul* 148

Target Center, *Minneapolis* 148

WINTER FUN
Afton Alps, *Hastings*. 149

Buck Hill, *Burnsville* 149

Giants Ridge Golf & Ski Resort, *Biwabik*. 149

Green Acres Recreational (Snow Tubing), *Lake Elmo* 149

Hyland Ski & Snowboard Area, *Bloomington* 149

Lutsen Mountains, *Lutsen* 150

Mount Kato Ski Area, *Mankato* 150

Spirit Mountain, *Duluth* 150

Welch Village, *Welch* 150

Wild Mountain, *Taylors Falls* 150

HAUNTED MINNESOTA

There's only one thing better than sitting around a campfire telling ghost stories, and that's actually exploring Minnesota's own haunted sites.

1 Fitzgerald Theater

10 East Exchange Street, St. Paul; 651-290-1200; www.fitzgeraldtheater.org

Two ghosts.

2 Forepaugh's Restaurant

276 South Exchange Street, St. Paul; 651-224-5606; www.forepaughs.com

At least one ghost.

3 Guthrie Theater

818 South 2nd Street, Minneapolis; 612-377-2224 or 877-447-8243; www.guthrietheater.org

At least one ghost.

4 Minneapolis City Hall

350 South 5th Street, Minneapolis; 612-596-9512; www.municipalbuildingcommission.org

At least one ghost.

NOTE: The City Hall Carillon Committee holds bell concerts regularly at the Minneapolis City Hall. Check website for schedule.

5 Ramsey County Courthouse

15 West Kellogg Boulevard, St. Paul; 651-266-8002; www.ramseycounty.us

Multiple ghosts.

6 St. John's University

P.O. Box 2000, Collegeville; 320-363-2011; www.csbsju.edu

Multiple ghosts.

7 St. Mary's College

700 Terrace Heights, Winona; 507-452-4430 or 800-635-5987

One nasty ghost.

8 The Palace Theatre

104 East Main and North Freeman, Luverne; www.palacetheatre.us

Two ghosts.

MINNESOTA'S FORGOTTEN FOREST

9 The Lost Forty

From Bemidji, take Highway 71 north to County 30 east (which turns into County 13). At the T, turn left onto Highway 46 (north), then east on County 29; turn north onto County 26.

Minnesota has its own Bermuda Triangle of sorts, known as The Lost Forty. This is 40 acres of virgin forest, originally missing from the state's tally of total acreage.

You'll find The Lost Forty in the Chippewa National Forest, approximately 50 miles northeast of Bemidji. Picturesque hiking trails through mature white pines, maples and oaks.

OPTION

Since you're in the neighborhood, stop in at **Hafeman Boat Works** to watch the nearly lost art of birch bark canoe making. Ray Boessel Jr. constructs canoes ranging in size from 5–26 feet long, turning out one per week during the summer months. His wife's grandfather started the business in 1921. Located at 59520 Highway 6, Bigfork; 218-743-3709.

SCENIC BYWAYS

To help you find those great views, Minnesota designated over 2,000 miles of roads as scenic byways. For more information, call the Minnesota Office of Tourism at 888-VISITMN (888-847-4866) or 651-296-5029; www.exploreminnesota.com. Metro Square: 121 7th Place East, Suite 100, St. Paul.

10 Apple Blossom Drive

19 miles

Travel a loop south off of Highway 61 through the Richard J. Dorer Memorial Hardwood Forest down to La Crescent—the Apple Capital of Minnesota. Numerous bluff orchards with spring apple blossoms and brilliant fall color.

11 Avenue of Pines

46 miles

Largely undeveloped, this rustic, paved road carves through lakes, marshes and a pine forest. It also crosses the Laurentian Divide, the point separating the waters that flow north to Hudson Bay and south into the Mississippi. Route travels Highway 46 from Deer River to Northome.

12 Edge of the Wilderness

46 miles

From Grand Rapids to Effie on Highway 38, you'll explore a region thick with lakes, and the Chippewa National Forest—home to some of the highest densities of Bald Eagles in the lower 48 states.

13 Glacial Ridge Trail

220 miles

From Willmar to Alexandria, explore a rolling terrain of lakes, woodlands and farmland.

14 Grand Rounds

53 miles

One of only a handful of urban national scenic byways, Grand Rounds follows parkways in a loop through Minneapolis, skirting the chain of lakes on the west side. See the famous Stone Arch Bridge and Minnehaha Falls.

15 Great River Road

562 miles

The Great River Road follows the Mississippi River from its birthplace at Itasca State Park, winding all the way south to the Iowa border. Many quaint and interesting river towns along this route including Aitkin, Little Falls, Monticello, Hastings, Red Wing, Wabasha and Winona.

16 Gunflint Trail

57 miles

Highway 12 travels from the scenic harbor town of Grand Marais inland through the rolling hills of Superior National Forest. The Gunflint Trail borders the Boundary Waters Canoe Area Wilderness. Besides bird watching, this road is a great place to see deer, moose, bear and wolves.

17 Historic Bluff Country

88 miles

Highway 16 heading west from La Crescent to Dexter offers sweeping views, picture-perfect trout streams, limestone cliffs, Forestville/Mystery Cave State Park and charming villages.

18 Lady Slipper

28 miles

Cut through the western side of the Chippewa National Forest on Highway 39 from Blackduck to Cass Lake. A blend of pine, aspen and birch forests, lakes, wetlands, hayfields and bogs.

19 Lake Country

88 miles

This North Woods drive takes in the lake country between Detroit Lakes and Walker on Highway 34, with a short jaunt north from Park Rapids to Itasca State Park on Highway 71. Lots of pine/hardwood forests and numerous lakes interspersed with some farmland.

20 Minnesota River Valley

300 miles

From Belle Plaine, the Minnesota River Valley dips south to Mankato before heading northwest to Browns Valley. Take in some of the state's best farmland, as well as some of the oldest rock in the world (3.5 billion years).

21 North Shore

154 miles

From Duluth to the Canadian border, travel scenic Highway 61 along Lake Superior for lighthouses, eight state parks with tons of water-falls and hiking, giant ore freighters, historical towns, fish boils, a reconstruction of a late-1700s fur-trading post and so much more.

22 Otter Trail

150 miles

A circular route through rolling hills thick with maple, oak, birch and more than 1,000 lakes. Very colorful fall drive. Fergus Falls area.

23 Paul Bunyan

48 miles

According to one Paul Bunyan tall tale, the puddles left behind by the giant lumberjack's footprints became Minnesota's 10,000 lakes. Two loops on country roads explore the area north of Brainerd.

24 Rushing Rapids

9 miles

This short, awe-inspiring drive on Highway 210 winds along the St. Louis River through Jay Cooke State Park. While no longer an "official" scenic byway, it offers incredible views. Don't miss seeing the gorge from a swinging suspension bridge.

25 Shooting Star

28 miles

Travel Highway 56 from the Iowa border heading northwest through Lake Louise State Park, over to Rose Creek. This is prairie and wildflower country much as it was when the first settlers came to the region.

26 Skyline Parkway

38 miles

Follow a ridgeline high above Duluth for breathtaking views of Lake Superior and the Duluth harbor.

27 Veterans Evergreen Memorial

50 miles

Highway 23 from Askov to Duluth is a mix of farmland and woods, crisscrossed by meandering creeks. Great fall colors.

28 Waters of the Dancing Sky

191 miles

Named for the shimmering northern lights, this is the state's northernmost byway. Following Highway 11 from Karlstad to International Falls, travel this route of lakes, woods, small towns and farmland.

SPORTS

Call the numbers listed below for schedules and ticket information.

29 Canterbury Park (Horse Racing)

1100 Canterbury Road, Shakopee; 952-445-RACE (952-445-7223) or
800-340-6361; www.canterburypark.com

30 Minnesota Lynx WNBA Basketball

Target Center, 601 1st Avenue North, Minneapolis; 612-673-8400;
lynx.wnba.com

31 Minnesota Timberwolves Basketball

Target Center, 601 1st Avenue North, Minneapolis; 612-673-1234;
www.nba.com/timberwolves

32 Minnesota Twins Baseball

Target Field, Minneapolis; 800-33TWINS (800-338-9467); twins.mlb.com

33 Minnesota Vikings Football

U.S. Bank Stadium, downtown Minneapolis; 800-745-3000; www.vikings.com

34 Minnesota Wild NHL Hockey

Xcel Energy Center, 175 West Kellogg Boulevard, St. Paul; 651-222-WILD
(651-222-9453); wild.nhl.com

35 Running Aces Harness Park (Horse Racing)

15201 Running Aces Boulevard, Columbus; 651-925-4600; www.runaces.com

36 St. Paul Saints Baseball

CHS Field, St. Paul; 651-644-6659; www.saintsbaseball.com

37 University of Minnesota Athletics

University of Minnesota, Twin Cities Campus, Minneapolis; 612-624-8080 or
800-UGOPHER (800-846-7437); www.gophersports.com

TWIN CITIES THEATER & MUSIC

The Twin Cities has one of the highest numbers of theaters per capita in the country. Check with the theater listed for shows, times and tickets.

38 Brave New Workshop

824 Hennepin Avenue, Minneapolis; 612-332-6620;
www.bravenewworkshop.com

Comedy and satire performances year-round.

39 Chanhassen Dinner Theatres

501 West 78th Street, Chanhassen; 952-934-1525; www.chanhassendt.com

Largest professional dinner theater company in the country with performances year-round. Wheelchair accessible.

40 Children's Theatre Company

2400 3rd Avenue South, Minneapolis; 612-874-0400;
www.childrenstheatre.org

Wheelchair accessible.

41 Fitzgerald Theater

10 East Exchange Street, St. Paul; 651-290-1200;
www.fitzgeraldtheater.publicradio.org

Home of "A Prairie Home Companion" radio show. Full schedule of concerts and performances.

42 Guthrie Theater

818 South 2nd Street, Minneapolis; 612-377-2224 or 877-447-8243;
www.guthrietheater.org

Performances year-round. Wheelchair accessible.

43 Historic State and Orpheum Theatres

Hennepin Avenue between 8th and 10th Streets South, Minneapolis.
800-982-2787; www.hennepintheatretrust.org

Broadway touring shows and variety of concerts.
Wheelchair accessible.

44 History Theatre

30 East 10th Street, St. Paul; 651-292-4323; www.historytheatre.com

Wheelchair accessible.

45 Orchestra Hall

1111 Nicollet Mall, Minneapolis; 612-371-5656; www.minnesotaorchestra.org

Home to Minnesota Orchestra. Wheelchair accessible.

46 Ordway Music Theatre

345 Washington Street, St. Paul; 651-224-4222; www.ordway.org

Home to the St. Paul Chamber Orchestra and Minnesota Opera, with full schedule of other concerts and touring shows. Wheelchair accessible.

47 Park Square Theatre Company

20 West 7th Place, St. Paul; 651-291-7005; www.parksquaretheatre.org

Wheelchair accessible.

48 Penumbra Theatre Company

270 North Kent Street, St. Paul; 651-224-3180; www.penumbratheatre.org

The only professional black theater group in Minnesota. Presents the Black Nativity each holiday season as well as August Wilson plays.

49 Target Center

600 1st Avenue North, Minneapolis; 612-673-0900; www.targetcenter.com

Concerts, performances and sporting events, including Timberwolves and Lynx basketball. Wheelchair accessible.

WINTER FUN

Some of the best things about Minnesota are the changing seasons. As the saying goes, "If you don't like the weather we're having now, wait one minute."

Winter brings new opportunities for fun and adventure. The parks system offers sliding, snowshoeing, cross-country skiing, ice skating and snowmobiling. Over 10,000 frozen lakes provide great ice fishing. Pick up snowmobile trail maps at information centers or rural area businesses.

50 Afton Alps

6600 Peller Avenue South, Hastings (15 miles east of St. Paul); 800-328-1328 or 651-436-5245; www.aftonalps.com

5 chalets, 18 lifts, 48 runs.

51 Buck Hill

15400 Buck Hill Road, Burnsville; 952-435-7174; www.buckhill.com

Chalet, 8 lifts, 16 runs.

52 Giants Ridge Golf & Ski Resort

6329 Wynne Creek Drive, Biwabik; 800-688-7669 or 218-865-3000; www.giantsridge.com

35 alpine runs, 36 miles of groomed cross-country ski trails, access to more than 2,000 miles of groomed snowmobile trails, resort lodging, entertainment, two 18-hole golf courses.

53 Green Acres Recreational (Snow Tubing)

8989 North 55th Street, Lake Elmo (off Highway 36); 651-770-6060; www.greenacresrec.com

Chalet with concessions, 2 hills, 3 rope tows. Inner tubes provided. Call or check website for hours.

54 Hyland Ski & Snowboard Area

8800 Chalet Road, Bloomington; 763-694-7800; www.hylandski.com

Chalet, 3 lifts, 12 runs.

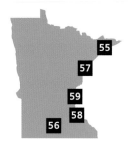

55 Lutsen Mountains

467 Ski Hill Road, Lutsen; 218-663-7281; www.lutsen.com

95 mountain runs (1,000-foot vertical drop), chalet, restaurant, resort lodging, summer hiking and the Alpine Slide—an exhilarating sled ride on a half mile of twisting, turning track. Lutsen's new state-of-the-art gondola ride is the only one in the Midwest.

56 Mount Kato Ski Area

20461 Highway 66, Mankato; 800-668-5286 or 507-625-3363; www.mountkato.com

Chalet, 8 lifts, 3 handle tows, 19 runs.

57 Spirit Mountain

9500 Spirit Mountain Place, Duluth; 800-642-6377; www.spiritmt.com

Chalet, 5 lifts, 22 runs (700-foot vertical drop).

58 Welch Village

South of the Metro near Welch. Take the Welch Village Road from Highway 61; 651-258-4567; www.welchvillage.com

2 chalets, 9 lifts, 50 runs.

59 Wild Mountain

Highway 16, Taylors Falls; 651-465-6315; www.wildmountain.com

Chalet, 4 lifts, 23 runs.

Rushing Rapids scenic byway, Jay Cooke State Park

Index

100-Mile Garage Sale, Wabasha, 100

A

Aamodt's Hot Air Balloon Rides,
    Stillwater, 87
Abigail's Attic Antiques &
    Collectibles, Akeley, 101
Adourn antiques, Chatfield, 105
Afton Alps, Hastings, 149
Akeley, 30, 101
Alexander Ramsey Park, Redwood Falls, 46
Alexandria, 130, 142
Alexis Bailly Vineyard, Hastings, 133
Alma, WI, 99, 113
Al's Antique Mall, Red Wing, 96
American Indian petroglyphs, 38
American Swedish Institute, Minneapolis, 74
Amish Buggy Byway, Highway 52, 66
Amish tours, 66, 108
Amnicon Falls State Park, 122
ancient carvings, 38
Angel Hill Historic District, Taylors Falls, 89
antiquing day trips, 92–109
Apple Blossom Drive, 142
Apple Valley Gifts & Antiques,
    La Crescent, 103
August Schell Brewery, New Ulm, 56, 131
Austin, 108–109
Avenue of Pines, Highway 46, 142
Avian Acres Wild Bird Supply, Eagle Bluff, 45
A-Z Collectibles, Winona, 102

B

Bailiwick antiques, Chatfield, 105
Baptism River, 124
Barn Bluff, Red Wing, 113
Basilica of Saint Mary, 10
Basil's, Highway 35, 97
Battle Creek Park, Maplewood, 66
Bauer, Mary M., 2
Bauer, Steve and Sylvia, 8
Bay City, WI, 97
Bay Point Park, Red Wing, 112
Bayfront Carriages, Duluth, 22
Bayfront Festival Park, 17
Bell Museum of Natural History,
    Minneapolis, 74
Bemidji, 30, 44
Benton, Thomas Hart, 76
Bergquist Pioneer Cabin, Moorhead, 73
Big Lake Wilderness Lodge, Ely, 47–48
Big Ole, Alexandria, 130

Birch Coulee Battlefield, Morton, 46
Biwabik, 63, 64, 149
Blakeslee Field, Minnesota
    State University, 132
Blandin Paper Mill, Grand Rapids, 60
Blue Mounds State Park, 37, 38
Boathouse Village, Red Wing, 113
Boessel, Ray Jr., 141
Bonanzaville, West Fargo, ND, 72
Boundary Country Trekking, Grand Marais, 28
Boundary Waters Canoe Area Wilderness, 28
Brainerd, 30, 43, 44, 144
Brave New Workshop, Minneapolis, 147
breweries of Twin Cities, 134
Brule River, 125
Buck Hill, Burnsville, 149
Buena Vista Park, Alma WI, 99, 113
Bunyan, Paul, 30, 44, 144
buses in Twin Cities, 3
Butler, Eloise, 53

C

Cabela's outdoor retail center, 39–40
Cannon Falls, 97, 106, 121
Cannon River tubing, 38–39
Cannon River Winery, 106
Cannon Valley Trail, Cannon Falls, 121
Cannon Valley Trail, Red Wing, 97
Canterbury Park (horse racing), 146
Caponi Art Park, Eagan, 52
Caribou Coffee, Red Wing, 112
Caribou Falls Wayside,
    Tettegouche State Park, 125
Carlos Creek Winery, Alexandria, 130
Cascade Bay Water Park, Eagan, 45
Cascade Falls, Osceola, 115
Cascade River State Park, Lutsen, 118, 125
Cass Lake, 30, 143
Cathedral of St. Paul, 6, 9
caves, 65–67
Chamber of Commerce, St. Paul and
    Minneapolis, 3
Chanhassen Dinner Theatres, 147
Charles A. Lindbergh House, Little Falls, 43
Chatfield, 105
children's museums, 41, 60, 72
Children's Museum at Yunker Farm,
    Fargo, ND, 72
Children's Theatre Company, Minneapolis, 147
Chippewa National Forest, 141, 142, 143
Chocolate Shoppe, Mantorville, 82
Church of Saint Agnes, St. Paul, 9
Church of the Assumption, St. Paul, 10
churches, day trips to, 6–11
Churn Dash Antiques, Rochester, 105

Clemens, Bill, 57
Clemens Rose Gardens, St. Cloud, 57
commuter trains in Twin Cities, 3
Commonweal Theatre Company,
    Lanesboro, 104
Como Park Zoo, St. Paul, 42, 54
Como-Harriet Streetcar Line, 114
Comstock, Senator Solomon G., 72
Comstock House, Moorhead, 72
Congdon, Elisabeth, 19
Convention & Visitors Bureau, St. Paul, 4
Convention & Visitors Association,
    Minneapolis, 3
cottonwood, Minnesota's largest, 47
Country Side Antique Mall,
    Cannon Falls, 106
Cross River Falls, Schroeder, 125
Crystal Cave, Spring Valley, WI, 67

D

Danzinger Vineyards, Alma, WI, 99
day trip themes
    churches, 6–11
    Duluth, 12, 25
    Extreme Adventures, 26–33
    Family Day, 34–49
    Garden Tours, 50–57
    Geology & Cave Tours, 58–69
    Museums, Historic Sites & the Arts, 70–77
    Odds & Ends, 136–151
    Rochester, 78–83
    Romantic Getaways, 84–91
    Small Town Antiquing, 92–109
    Trains, Trains & More Trains, 110–117
    Waterfalls, 118–127
    Wine & Beer Lovers' Tours, 128–135
Dempsey, Jack, 126
Depot, Duluth, 20
Dorothy Molter Cabin Museum, Ely, 48
Dougherty's Rainy Lake Houseboats,
    Voyageurs National Park, 32
Douglas Lodge, 30
Duluth day trips, 12–25
Duluth Huskies baseball, 16
Duluth Waterfront Tours, 31

E

Eagle Bluff Environmental Learning Center,
    Lanesboro, 44
Eau Galle Dam, Spring Valley, WI, 67
Ebel's Voyageur Houseboats,
    Voyageurs National Park, 32
Edge of the Wilderness, Highway 38, 142
Edmund Fitzgerald shipwreck, 12
Eli Wirtanen Pioneer Farm,
    Biwabik, 64

Eloise Butler Wildflower Garden & Bird
    Sanctuary, Minneapolis, 53
Enger Park, Duluth, 24
Enger Tower, Duluth, 25
Englishman's Carriage House B&B,
    Stillwater, 88
Excelsior day trips, 86, 115
Excelsior Streetcar Line, 86, 115
Extreme Adventures day trips, 26–33
Eyota, 107
Eyota Antiques, Highway 14, 107

F

Fairlawn Mansion, Duluth, 18
Falconer Vineyards, Red Wing, 113
Family Day day trips, 34–49
Fargo-Moorhead Visitors' Center,
    Fargo, ND, 73
Farmamerica, 39
Finn Creek Open Air Museum,
    New York Mills, 117
Fire & Ice, Alma, WI, 99
Fitger's Brewery Complex, Duluth, 22
Fitger's Brewery Complex Museum,
    Duluth, 19
Fitger's Brewhouse Brewery & Grille,
    Duluth, 22
Fitger's Wine Cellars, Duluth, 22
Fitzgerald Theater, St. Paul, 140, 147
Flat Pennies Ice Cream, Bay City, WI, 97
Flower Valley Vineyard, Red Wing, 113
Folsom, W. H. C., 88
Folsom House, Taylors Falls, 88–89
Forepaugh's Restaurant, St. Paul, 140
Forest History Center, Grand Rapids, 60
Forestville, Historic, 104
Forestville/Mystery Cave State Park, 65
Fort Ridgely, Fairfax, 46
Fort Snelling, St. Paul, 70, 74–75
Fountain, 104
Franconia Sculpture Park, Taylors Falls, 89
Frederick R. Weisman Art Museum,
    Minneapolis, 75
Freight House Restaurant, Stillwater, 87

G

Garden Tours day trips, 50–57
Garland, Judy, 60
Garvin Heights, Winona, 102
Gasthaus Bavarian Hunter Restaurant,
    Stillwater, 133
Geology & Cave Tours day trips, 58–69
Giants Ridge Golf & Ski Resort, Biwabik, 149
Gibbs Farm, St. Paul, 34, 41
Gilfillan Estate, Redwood Falls, 55
Glacial Ridge Trail, 142

Glen iron mine, 62
Glensheen, Duluth, 19
Gondola Romantica, Stillwater, 87
Gooseberry Falls State Park, Two Harbors, 123
Grand Portage National Monument, 126
Grand Portage State Park, Grand Portage, 126
Grand Rounds, Minneapolis, 143
Grand Slam Sports, Burnsville, 45
Grandma's Restaurant, Duluth, 21
Great American Think-Off, New York Mills, 117
Great Lakes Aquarium, Duluth, 16
Great River Houseboats, Alma, WI, 99
Great River Road, 30, 96–100, 143
Green Acres Recreational (snow tubing), 149
Greenery Café & Bakery, Duluth, 22
Greyhound Bus Museum, Hibbing, 62
Gunflint Lodge, Grand Marias, 29
Gunflint Trail, Grand Marias, 125, 143
Gustavus Adolphus College, 55
Guthrie Theater, Minneapolis, 140, 147

H

Hafeman Boat Works, Big Fork, 141
Harley Trip to the Headwaters,
   Minneapolis, 29–30
Harmony, 65, 66, 108
Hassam, Childe, 76
Hastings, 8, 121, 133, 143, 149
haunted Minnesota, 140–141
Haunted Ship, Duluth, 20
Hawk Ridge Nature Reserve, Duluth, 24
Hay Creek Stables, Red Wing, 96
Heritage Antiques, Walker, 102
Heritage House Victorian Museum,
   Rochester, 80
Hibbing Historical Society Museum, 62
Hibbing Public Library, 62
Hibbing Taconite Company Mine Tour, 62
Highway 14 Route West—Eyota, 107
Highway 52 Route North—Oronoco, 105
Hill, James J., 75, 114
Hill Annex Mine State Park, Calumet, 61
Hill of Three Waters, 61
Historic 1916 Osceola Depot, 115
Historic Bluff Country, Highway 16, 143
Historic Corner Store, Alma, WI, 99
Historic Forestville, 65, 105
Historic State & Orpheum Theatres,
   Minneapolis, 147
Historical & Cultural Society of Clay County,
   Moorhead, 73
History Center of Olmsted County,
   Rochester, 82
History Theatre, St. Paul, 147
Hockey Hall of Fame Museum, Eveleth, 63

Hopperstad Norwegian Stave Church,
   Moorhead, 73
Hormel family, 108
horse racing, 146
House of Hidden Treasure, St. Charles, 107
Houston, 103
Houston Nature Center, 103
Hoyt Lakes, 60, 64
Hubbell House, Mantorville, 82
Hull Rust Mahoning Mine, Hibbing, 61
Hyland Sky & Snowboard Area,
   Bloomington, 149

I

Inspiration Peak, Brandon, 130
International Band Music Lending Library,
   Chatfield, 105
International Owl Center, Houston, 103
International Wolf Center, Ely, 48
Interstate State Park, Taylors Falls, 89
Iron Range Research Library & Archives,
   Chisholm, 62
Iron Trail, Biwabik, 63
Isle Royale National Park, Grand Portage, 126
Itasca State Park, 29

J

J&J Barbecue, Pepin, WI, 98
Jackson Street Roundhouse, St. Paul, 114
JailHouse Historic Inn, Preston, 104
James J. Hill House, Minneapolis, 75
Jay C. Hormel Nature Center, Austin, 108
Jay Cooke State Park, Carlton, 17, 145
Jeffers Petroglyphs Comfrey, 38
JJ Astor Restaurant & Lounge, Duluth, 23
John Kruesel's General Merchandise,
   Rochester, 105
Judge C. R. Magney State Park,
   Grand Marais, 125
Judy Garland Children's Museum,
   Grand Rapids, 60
Just So antiques, Chatfield, 105

K

Karpeles Manuscript Library Museum,
   Duluth, 19
Kensington Runestone Museum,
   Alexandria, 130
kids, see children

L

La Crescent, 103, 142
Lady Slipper, Chippewa National Forest, 143
Lake Bemidji State Park, 30
Lake Country, Highway 34, 144

Lake Louise State Park, 145
Lake Park, Winona, 103
Lake Superior, 12, 16, 20, 24, 31, 122, 123,
    124, 125, 144
Lake Superior Maritime Visitor Center,
    Duluth, 16, 123
Lake Superior Zoo, Duluth, 17
Lake Vermillion-Soudan Underground Mine
    State Park, 64
Landing, the, Shakopee, 77
Lanesboro, 104
Lantern Antiques, Pine Island, 106
Lardner, Ring, 126
Laurentian Divide, 142
Lee, Jann & Roger, 116
Leif Erickson Park, 15, 22
Leif Erickson Park & the Greenery Café &
    Bakery, Duluth, 22
Leonidas Overlook, Eveleth, 63
Levee Park, Red Wing, 112
Lewis, Sinclair, 130
light rail in Twin Cities, 3
Lighthouse Point, Two Harbors, 124
Lindbergh, Charles, 3, 43, 107
Lind's Recycled Goods, Park Rapids, 101
Linnaeus Arboretum & Sculpture Garden,
    St. Peter, 55
Little Log House Village, Hastings, 8
Little River General Store, Lanesboro, 104
Lock and Dam No. 4, Highway 35, 113
Lone Pine Antiques, Alma, 99
Longyear Drill Site, Hoyt Lakes, 64
Loring Park, St. Paul, 10
Lost Forty, the, 141
Lowell Inn, Stillwater, 88
Lower Sioux Agency, Redwood Falls, 47
Lutsen Mountains, 150
Lyndale Rose Garden, Minneapolis, 53

M
Mabel, 107
Maiden Rock, WI, 97–98
Mall of America, Bloomington, 42–43
Mankato, 131–132, 144, 150
Mankato Mdewakanton Powwow, 132
Mantorville, 109
Mantorville, Historic, 82
Mantorville Theatre Company, 83
Maris, Roger, 73
Marjorie McNeely Conservatory,
    St. Paul, 50, 53–54
Masqueray, Emmanuel Louis, 9
Mayo, Drs. William J. & Charles H., 80
Mayo, W. W., 55
Mayo Clinic Hospital, Rochester, 78, 80

Mayo Park & Arboretum, Le Sueur, 55
Mayowood Mansion, Rochester, 80
McAlpine, Ardele, 101
Memorabilia Antiques, Mantorville, 83, 109
Memorial Park, Red Wing, 113
Mesabi Iron Range, 60–64
Mesabi Railway Trolley, Chisholm, 62
metro transit in Twin Cities, 3
metroConnections' guided tours, 3
Mickey's Diner, St. Paul, 10
Midwest Motorcycle, Minneapolis, 29
Mill City Museum, Minneapolis, 120
Minneapolis, information and tours about, 3
Minneapolis City Hall, 140
Minneapolis Institute of Art, 75
Minneapolis Sculpture Garden, 10, 54, 77
Minnehaha Depot, Minneapolis, 110, 114, 121
Minnehaha Falls, Minneapolis, 121, 127, 143
Minneopa State Park, Mankato, 132
Minnesota Children's Museum, St. Paul, 41
Minnesota Discovery Center, Chisholm, 62
Minnesota Fishing Museum & Hall of Fame,
    Little Falls, 43
Minnesota History Center, St. Paul, 75–76
Minnesota Landscape Arboretum,
    Chanhassen, 52–53
Minnesota Lynx WNBA basketball,
    Minneapolis, 146
Minnesota Museum of American Art,
    St. Paul, 76
Minnesota Museum of Mining, Chisholm, 63
Minnesota River Valley, 144
Minnesota State Capitol, St. Paul, 76
Minnesota State University,
    Blakeslee Field, 132
Minnesota Timberwolves basketball,
    Minneapolis, 146
Minnesota Twins baseball, Minneapolis, 146
Minnesota Vikings football, Minneapolis, 146
Minnesota Vikings training camp,
    Mankato, 132
Minnesota Whitewater, Duluth, 17
Minnesota Wild NHL hockey, St. Paul, 146
Minnesota Zoo, Apple Valley, 42
Mississippi River, 29, 66, 120, 143
Mississippi train tracking, 112–113
Molter, Dorothy, 48
Mom's Antique Mall, Oronoco, 106
Morgan Creek Vineyards, New Ulm, 131
Morton gneiss, 47
Mount Kato Ski Area, Mankato, 132, 150
Mountain Iron mine, 63
Mower County Historical Society, Austin, 109
Muddy Waters, Prescott, WI, 90
Munsinger Gardens, St. Cloud, 57

Museums, Historic Sites & the Arts
    day trips, 70–77
music and theaters, 147–148
Mystery Cave, Preston, 65

N

Naniboujou Lodge, Grand Marais, 126
National Eagle Center, Wabasha, 49, 100
Nelson, Ross, 39
Nelson, WI, 98
Nevis, 101
New Ulm Glockenspiel, 131
New York Mills, 116
New York Mills Regional Cultural
    Center, 116–117
Niagara Cave, Harmony, 58, 65–66
Nickelodeon Universe, Bloomington, 43
Noerenberg Memorial Gardens, Orono, 55
North Hibbing, 61
North Shore, Highway 61, 144
North Shore Scenic Drive, 123–126
North Shore Scenic Railroad, Duluth, 17, 23
North Shore Scenic Railroad—Pizza Train,
    Duluth, 17
Northern Vineyards, Stillwater, 133
Northernaire Houseboats, Voyageurs
    National Park, 32
Nugget Lake County Park, Plum City, WI, 68

O

Odds & Ends day trips, 136–151
Official Visitors Guides, 4
Olcott House Bed & Breakfast Inn, Duluth, 23
Old Firehouse & Police Museum, Duluth, 21
Old Frontenac Historic District, Wabasha, 100
Old Jail Bed & Breakfast, Taylors Falls, 89
Old Log Theater, Excelsior, 86
Old Mill Restaurant, Austin, 109
Old Rooster Antiques, Oronoco, 106
Oldstuff, Bay City, WI, 97
Oliver H. Kelley Farm, Elk River, 76
Olmsted County, History Center of, 82
On the River Boutique, Wabasha, 100
Orchestra Hall, Minneapolis, 148
Ordway Music Theatre, St. Paul, 148
Oronoco, 105–106
Orr Bog Walk, Orr, 33
Osceola & St. Croix Valley Railway,
    Osceola, 89, 115
Otter Trail, Fergus Falls, 144
owls, 49, 103
Oxbow Park, Byron, 82

P

Padelford Riverboats, Harriet Island, 66–67
Palace Theatre, Luverne, 141
Palisade Head Cliffs,
    Tettegouche State Park, 124
Park Rapids, 101
Park Square Theatre Company, St. Paul, 148
Pattison, Martin, 18
Pattison State Park, 123
Paul Bunyan, Brainerd, 144
Paul Bunyan Trail, Brainerd to
    Bemidji, 44, 144
Pease Wildlife Museum, Chatfield, 105
Pepin, WI, 98
Peterson's Antiques & Stripping,
    Rochester, 105
petroglyphs, 38
Phelphs Mill, Alexandria, 130
Pickwick Mill, Winona, 103
Pine Grove Zoo, Little Falls, 44
Pine Island, 106
Playfront Park, Duluth, 17
Plummer, Dr. Henry S., 81
Plummer Building, Rochester, 80
Plummer House of the Arts, Rochester, 81
Port Town Trolley, Duluth, 22
Pottery Place Antiques, Red Wing, 96
Prescott, WI, day trips, 90
Preston, 66, 104
Proud's Bridgeside Antiques, Wabasha, 100

Q

Quarry Hill Nature Center, Rochester, 81

R

Radisson Hotel Duluth—Harborview, 23
Ramsey County Courthouse, St. Paul, 140
Raptor Center, St. Paul, 49
Red Wing, 96, 97, 112, 113, 131, 143
Red Wing Shoe Store, Red Wing, 96
Red Wing Stoneware Company, Red Wing, 96
Red Wing Visitors & Convention Bureau, 112
Redwood County Museum,
    Redwood Falls, 56
Renaissance Festival, Shakopee, 77
Renegade Theater Company, Duluth, 23
Richard J. Dorer Memorial
    Hardwood Forest, 142
Rieck's Lake Park, Alma, WI, 99
Rochester, 78–83, 105
Rochester Art Center, 81
Rochester Carillon bells, 80
Rochester day trips, 78–83
Rock Climb & Sea Kayak, Duluth, 31
Roger Maris Museum, Fargo, 73

Romantic Getaways day trips, 84–91
Room to Roam Farm Vacations,
    Fountain City, 31
Rourke Art Museum, Moorhead, 74
Running Aces Harness Park
    (horse racing), 146
Rush River Produce, Bay City, WI, 97
Rushing Rapids, Highway 210, 145
Ruth, Babe, 73, 126

S

Saint Croix Vineyards, 133
sandpaper museum, Two Harbors, 124
Sarah's Uniques & Jim's "MAN"tiques,
    St. Charles, 107
Scenic Byway County 39, 30
scenic byways, 142–145
Schaffer's Antiques, Cannon Falls, 106
Schurke, Paul, 33
Science Museum of Minnesota, S. Paul, 41
Shooting Star Scenic Byway, Austin, 108, 145
Sibley, Henry, 76
Sibley Historic Site, Mendota, 76–77
Sibley Park, Mankato, 132
Silver Lake Park, Rochester, 81
Six-Toed Cat Antiques, Park Rapids, 101
skiing, 149–150
Skyline Parkway, Duluth, 24, 145
Slim's Woodshed and Museum, Harmony, 108
Small Town Antiquing day trips, 92–109
Smiling Pelican Bakeshop,
    Maiden Rock, WI, 97
snow tubing, 149
Sod House on the Prairie, Sanborn, 40
Soudan Underground Mine State Park, 64
Spam Museum, Austin, 108
Split Rock Lighthouse, Lake Superior, 124
Split Rock Lighthouse State Park, 31, 124
Spoonbridge and Cherry Sculpture,
    Minneapolis, 54
sports venues, 146
Spring Grove, 107
Spring Valley, 65
S.S. *Meteor* Maritime Museum, Duluth, 20
S.S. *William A. Irvin* Ore Boat Museum, 20
St. Anthony Falls, Minneapolis, 120
St. Boniface Church, Hastings, 8
St. Charles, 106
St. Croix River, 84, 89, 91
St. Croix valley, 133
St. Croix Valley Railway, 89
St. James Hotel, Red Wing, 97
St. John the Baptist Catholic Church,
    Vermillion, 8
St. John's University, 141

St. Joseph Miesville Catholic Church,
    Hastings, 8
St. Louis River, 145
St. Mary's Catholic Church, New Trier, 9
St. Mary's College, 141
St. Paul, information and tour about, 3
St. Paul Saints baseball, 146
Star Island, Cass Lake, 30
State DNR Fish Hatchery, Lanesboro, 45
Steam Engine Museum, Mabel, 107
Steamboat Minnehaha, Excelsior, 86
Stearns History Museum, St. Cloud, 57
Steger, Will, 33
Stillwater day trips, 87–88
Stillwater Trolley, 87
Stockholm, WI, 98
Stockholm Gardens, WI, 98
streetcars, 114–115
Stutrud, Mark, 134
Summerhill Farm, Park Rapids, 101
Summerset Outdoor Flea Market,
    Park Rapids, 101
Summit Brewing, St. Paul, 134
Sun Porch, Park Rapids, 101
Superior, 12, 20, 21
Superior Hiking Trail, 124

T

Taconite State Trail, Grand Rapids, 60
Tapio, Siffert & Wilhelmina, 117
Target Center, Minneapolis, 148
Target Field, Minneapolis, 136, 146
Taylors Falls day trips, 88–89
Temperance River State Park, Schroeder, 125
Tettegouche State Park, Silver Bay, 124
theaters and music, 147–148
Thomas Sadler Roberts Bird Sanctuary,
    Minneapolis, 53
Tom's Logging Camp, Duluth, 18
tours of Minneapolis, St. Paul, 3
Toys for Boys, Park Rapids, 101
trains, commuter, in Twin Cities, 3
Trains, Trains & More Trains day trips, 110–117
Treasures Under Sugar Loaf, Winona, 102
Trinity Church, Spring Grove, 107
Triple Divide, 61
Turnblad, Swan J., 74
Tweed Museum of Art, Duluth, 21
Twice As Nice Antiques & Collectibles,
    Austin, 108
Twin Cities
    breweries, 134
    churches, 8–11

U

UFO capital of the world, Spring Valley, WI, 68
Union Depot, St. Paul, 116
United States Hockey Hall of Fame Museum,
   Eveleth, 63
University of Minnesota athletics,
   Minneapolis, 146
Upper Sioux Agency State Park,
   Granite Falls, 47
U.S.-Dakota War of 1862, 47

V

Valleyfair Amusement Park, Shakopee, 49
Van Gundy's Elk Farm, Houston, 45
Vermillion Falls, Hastings, 121
Veterans Evergreen Memorial,
   Highway 23, 145
Viking ship replica, 73
Villa Maria Center, Wabasha, 100
Village of Yesteryear, Owatonna, 40
Vince Shute Wildlife Sanctuary, Voyageurs
   National Park, 32–33
Vine Park Brewing, St. Paul, 134
Vino in the Valley, Prescott, WI, 90
Vintage Treasures & Home Décor,
   St. Charles, 107
visitors guides, 4
Vista Fleet Harbor Cruises, Duluth, 18, 24
Voyagaire Lodge & Houseboats, 32
Voyageurs National Park, 26, 32
Voyageurs National Park houseboats, 32

W

W. W. Mayo House, Le Sueur, 55
Wabasha day trips, 100
Wabasha Discount Market, 100
Wabasha Street Caves, St. Paul, 66
Walker, 102
Walker Art Center, Minneapolis, 54, 77
Walnut Grove—Laura Ingalls
   Wilder Museum, 40–41
Waterfront Sculpture Walk, Duluth, 21
Waters of the Dancing Sky, Highway 11, 145
Welch Mill canoeing, tubing, 38–39
Welch Village, 150
Welcome & Heritage Center, Prescott, WI, 90
Whistle Stop Inn Bed & Breakfast,
   New York Mills, 116
Wild Mountain, Taylors Falls, 150
Wilder, Laura Ingalls, 40–41, 98
William A. Irvin (Haunted Ship), 20
Wine & Beer Lovers' Tours day trips, 128–135
Wine Cafe Pub & Eatery, Mankato, 131
Winona, 102–103
winter fun, 149–150

Wintergreen Dogsled Vacations, Ely, 33
Wisconsin Point, Superior, WI, 122
Wizard of Oz, Judy Garland's
   Children's Museum, 60
Wood, Grant, 76
Woodtick Musical Theater, 30
World's Largest Art Tractor,
   New York Mills, 117
Wright, Frank Lloyd, 67

Y

Yunker Farm, Children's Museum at, 72

Z

Zollman Zoo, Byron, 82
Zumbrota, 122